The Committed Reader

Reading for Utility, Pleasure, and Fulfillment in the Twenty-First Century

Robert A. Stebbins

THE SCARECROW PRESS, INC.
Lanham • Toronto • Plymouth, UK
2013

Published by Scarecrow Press, Inc.
A wholly owned subsidiary of The Rowman & Littlefield Publishing Group, Inc.
4501 Forbes Boulevard, Suite 200, Lanham, Maryland 20706
www.rowman.com

10 Thornbury Road, Plymouth PL6 7PP, United Kingdom

British Library Cataloguing in Publication Information Available

Library of Congress Cataloging-in-Publication Data

Stebbins, Robert A., 1938–
The committed reader : reading for utility, pleasure, and fulfillment in the twenty-first century /
Robert A. Stebbins.
p. cm.
Includes bibliographical references and index.
ISBN 978-0-8108-8596-7 (pbk. : alk. paper) — ISBN 978-0-8108-8597-4 (ebook)
1. Books and reading. I. Title.
Z1003.S833 2013
028—dc23
2012029039

♾™ The paper used in this publication meets the minimum requirements of American
National Standard for Information Sciences Permanence of Paper for Printed Library
Materials, ANSI/NISO Z39.48-1992.

Printed in the United States of America

To Landon, a testimony to the love of reading

Contents

Acknowledgments

My grandson Landon Nesbitt, to whom this book is dedicated, was a significant part of its inspiration. I have recognized for several years that leisure studies needed a book-length treatment of the liberal arts reading hobbies and that I should write such a work. While I was searching for the optimal literary facture with which to carry off this project, Landon, now 12 years old, had begun much earlier to show an extraordinary interest in reading first children's and then adolescents' books. His reading, classified here as pleasurable, occurs whenever he finds a few moments, lasts for hours if circumstances allow, and frequently has him shuffling between two or three novels. He loves to describe what he has just read and to consider how things might be different were the plot and its characters changed in certain ways. His books often trigger flights of imagination, one of the many types of casual leisure enjoyed in this genre of literature. In brief, though the present volume centers on adults, Landon showed me, even as a child, some of the essential features of committed reading. Turning to the editorial side of bringing this book into the world, I deeply appreciate the efforts that Martin Dillon, acquisitions editor, put into the project. They were at once efficient, knowledgeable, and always most friendly. And thanks, too, to Kellie Hagan, production editor, who took over from Martin, quickly and effectively moving the book to publication.

Introduction

I've never known any trouble that an hour's reading didn't assuage.
—Charles de Secondat

I declare after all there is no enjoyment like reading! How much sooner one tires of anything than of a book! When I have a house of my own, I shall be miserable if I have not an excellent library.
—Jane Austen

Happy is he who has laid up in his youth, and held fast in all fortune, a genuine and passionate love of reading.
—Rufus Choate

These three quotations valorize reading, no doubt about that. They also treat reading as though it concerned only certain kinds of literature. Thus, de Secondat, the eighteenth-century French philosopher also known as Montesquieu, might not be so assuaged if his hour's reading consisted of trying to decipher the fine print of an insurance policy or the instructions of how to assemble a complex piece of furniture from IKEA. Would Jane Austen, nineteenth-century English novelist, be so enamored of books were her library filled with cheap, popular novels? And Mr. Choate, a nineteenth-century lawyer and orator, might never have developed a passion for reading had he been forced, as a student, to read dull textbooks. In short, reading is a many-faceted activity, some of it enjoyable, some of it forced on us, some of it deeply rewarding, some of it bland and technical, some of it popular, and some of it esoteric.

This book looks into all these facets of reading and more. Its working definition of reading is that of the *Shorter Oxford English Dictionary* (SOED), sense 5: "the extent to which one reads or has read; literary knowledge." Acquiring a literary knowledge implies that such reading— call it *committed reading*—necessarily takes time and requires concentration. When we quickly glance at some printed material, we are not in this sense reading. Furthermore, there is no indication in this definition that reading is limited to the belles lettres, technical material, popular novels, newspapers, magazines, or any other type. Rather, it is all of this and more. Additionally, what the SOED definition fails to acknowledge is the existence of different types of reading material and the different motives for consuming it. I will consider the first under the headings of books, periodicals, pamphlets, and manuals. The second will be classified as utilitarian (including information seeking), pleasurable (including relaxa-

tion and escape), and fulfilling (including challenge, inspiration, and personal development). Finally, we shall see in chapter 1 that these types are
pursued across life's three domains of work, leisure, and non-work obligation. By the way, according to Clark and Rumbold (2006, p. 5), pleasurable reading, the most thoroughly analyzed of the three types, also goes
by an assortment of names, including "independent reading" (Cullinan,
2000), "voluntary reading" (Krashen, 2004), "leisure reading" (Greaney,
1980), "recreational reading" (Manzo and Manzo, 1995), and "ludic"
reading (Nell, 1988).

In fact, common usage distinguishes somewhat better than the SOED
the various kinds of reading available in modern times. When we say
something is a "good read," we are usually referring to enjoyable or
fulfilling material rather than something technical. However accurate
and concise the instructions to an IKEA sofa-bed, they are not a good
read, although they may be described as informative. Talk about reading
skills and the art of reading is actually a reference to technical and fine-
arts reading, since beyond the rudimentary skills acquired in school, neither capacity is needed to read popular material. As a third example
consider boring reading, a damning evaluation hurled by some students
at their assigned textbooks and supplementary readings. Neither are they
a good read.

So what are we doing when we consume a written passage that fails to
qualify as committed reading? One activity competent readers engage in
when not carefully reading written passages is skimming them. Such
cursory reading might be a prelude to a committed reading of the material,
an exploratory act to determine if a serious reading is in the participant's
interest. But it could also be a search for information, of the sort obtain-
able by a quick glance at the material. *Detailed ephemeral reading* is what
we do with complicated material that is, however, but a few pages in
length. Here we find such specimens as the IKEA instructions as well as
instructions on how to fill in a modern income tax form, set up a new
computer, and prepare an haute cuisine meal. We often engage in detailed ephemeral reading when we digest written material at an exhibit or
on a website. Finally, we sometimes engage in both types in the course of
consuming a short text like a newspaper article or a newsletter. We skim
this passage and carefully read the next one or even carefully reread the
one we just skimmed. No matter how we go about it, non-committed
reading is also an important way of gaining information, but to properly
examine such reading, would take us beyond the scope of the present
work.

These two are thus residual categories in this book, such that here
"reading" without qualifier will always refer to the committed variety.
That cursory and detailed ephemeral reading have been set aside in this
study is not to argue, however, that they are unimportant. Quite the
contrary. We are faced daily with all manner of reading material, some of

which can in a scanning be handled with dispatch. Further, there are also many routine situations in life where we must quickly read and understand quite ordinary but nevertheless detailed instructions. Skill at reading in general is also an aid to reading effectively and efficiently in these two areas. Nor will the two be wholly ignored; they will surface from time to time as context for this book, showing where committed reading leaves off and cursory or detailed ephemeral reading begins.

The world has been reading for millennia, though the practice only emerged with the invention of written language. The cuneiform and Elamite languages are believed to have been developed around 3300 BC, which were nevertheless practical creations intended to describe certain aspects of daily life. At this time language took the form of pictographs, with symbols or signs representing simple ideas such as a local animal, plant, or quantity of objects. Reading in this rudimentary language was strictly a practical act.

Reading as considered in this book began when written languages came to be used to communicate more complex ideas strung together to create a larger meaningful whole, whether a scientific observation, bit of commonsense information, artistic expression (poetry, stories), or philosophical or religious truth. Such reading is analyzed here as a special activity, during which the reader consumes written material enabling him to realize one or more particular ends, be they utilitarian, enjoyment, personal fulfillment, or a combination of these three. Furthermore, though most people use their eyes to read, we can certainly realize many of these ends by consuming the relevant material aurally, by hearing words originally set out to be read, or tactilely, by feeling text written in Braille. The larger point is that modern reading consists of understanding more or less complex ideas expressed, at least initially, in written language.

Yet, even today, reading is not the only way that people come to know the world in which they live. We occasionally observe certain symbols which communicate a great deal. Modern examples include a depiction of skull and crossbones (poison), a lit cigarette crossed out in various ways (no smoking), and the ubiquitous happy face. Pictures, sometimes said to be worth a thousand words, are not read but, as with symbols, are looked at and thereby, for the properly enculturated, understood. Additionally, we learn about our world from its familiar and unfamiliar sounds, feels, and smells, be they bird songs or ambulance sirens, earth tremors or heavy footfalls, cooking bacon or malodorant sewage. For people incapable of visual reading and unable to engage in aural or in Braille reading, the information and feelings provided by these other senses constitute their only contact with the physical world. Meanwhile, for the rest of us, reading is also important, albeit variously so.

That is, some people, though they know how to read, nonetheless read very little. They either prefer, or are forced, to learn about their world in other ways and to seek their leisure with minimal reliance on written words. They converse, listen to music, watch television programs produced to feature imagery (e.g., sportcasts, travelogues, graphic arts programs), and the like. Moreover, some people are unable to read. Some of them have poor, uncorrected, or uncorrectable vision. Some are illiterate, since reading is an acquired skill that they have not bothered to master sufficiently. Others are severly dyslectic and so they are unable to learn to read well. And still others are effectively illiterate, because the language they know is neither spoken nor published where they are presently living.

Since this book is about adult readers, sometimes including the committed late-teenage reader, the child reader will not be scrutinized here. Adult reading in all its manifestations has been much less studied, and it will take all the pages of this book to adequately cover the subject. Meanwhile, there is a voluminous literature on childhood reading, on how to improve it, inspire it, teach it, write material for it, and so on. The books listed on Amazon found under the search term of "reading" offer ample evidence of this. Some books for adults appear here as well, but most are manuals on how to read faster, build vocabulary, read in English as a second language, read for optimum comprehension, and similar interests.

The present book strikes out in a markedly different direction. It centers on reading as a special, goal-oriented activity pursued in all three domains of life, namely, work, leisure, and non-work obligation. Reading is in this framework conscious, purposive activity, the enactment of which requires concentration with the eyes (ears, fingers) focused intently on the material at hand. Nevertheless, we can engage in this activity while involved in certain parallel activities like waiting, resting, and riding somewhere (e.g., in an airplane, automobile, or subway car). Thus reading is often part of an individual's overall lifestyle, and depending on how much and what kind of it that person does, it may evolve into a special lifestyle all its own, as epitomized in the inveterate reader.

Voracious committed reading, it will be pointed out later, is not for everybody; some people love it to the point of making it a hobby, and others, among them many intellectuals, crave utilitarian information leading them to read assiduously for it but doing so mainly as a means to another end. What is the nature of the lifestyle created by so intense an interest? How is life organized socially and geographically around this kind of reading? How is reading distributed across life's three domains? Such questions are taken up in chapter 6. Before then we look into the theoretic basis of the study of reading set out in chapter 2 as the serious leisure perspective and the framework of library and information science. Chapter 3 examines the cultural and organizational background for reading, particularly as manifested in continuing and adult education and self-directed reading. Reading here is utilitarian, with some of it offering fulfillment as well. Casual leisure reading, or reading for pleasure, is the subject of chapter 4. In chapter 5 we consider the liberal arts hobbies, all of them centered largely, if not exclusively, on reading, a main outcome of which is personal development and self-fulfillment. But before tackling this to-do list, we need a sense of reading's situation in today's world.

ONE

Modern Reading

No entertainment is so cheap as reading, nor any pleasure so lasting.
—Lady Mary Wortley Montagu (1689–1762)

It is possible that, in Lady Montagu's day, utilitarian and popular, pleasurable reading were not to be found. So, given the material available for her consumption, this observation about reading's cheapness and durability helps explain the remarkable extent of the practice in modern times.

Jacobs (2011) holds that reading is alive and well in America, notwithstanding the alarm bells being sounded over supposedly insufficient reading, reading inappropriate material, and reading in the wrong way. He says that brick-and-mortar bookstores and their online counterparts have been hugely popular, even while the latter are threatening the existence of some of the former.[1] Oprah's Book Club, which ran from 1996 to May of 2011, was well recognized (as was its counterpart in Britain, the Richard and Judy Book Clubs; Styles, 2007, p. 5). A comparison of data for 1998 and 2008 on the proportions of book readers in the United States shows little change, with slightly over 40 percent of adults reading one book within a twelve-month period (U.S. Census Bureau, 2000, Table 437; U.S. Census Bureau 2010, Table 1203). Considering public library visits as another measure of the popularity of reading, the Institute of Museum and Library Services (2011, p. 7) reports in its 2009 survey that public library visitations in the United States had increased 24.3 percent since 2000. Moreover, the number of registered borrowers had risen by 4.8 percent from 2006, the first year such data were collected. Meanwhile in Canada "library usage transactions" rose 45 percent between 2000 and 2009 (Lumos Research, 2011). In England adult library visitations dropped about 9 percent between 2005 and 2008 and then remained steady through 2010 (Department of Culture, Media and Sport, 2010).

Nevertheless, the data gathered by the National Endowment for the Arts (NEA) are less sanguine. Gioia (2007) summarizes the findings set out in their report as they bear on the adult and late-teenage reader:

> The story the data tell is simple, consistent, and alarming. Although there has been measurable progress in recent years in reading ability at the elementary school level, all progress appears to halt as children enter their teenage years. There is a general decline in reading among teenage and adult Americans. Most alarming, both reading ability and the habit of regular reading have greatly declined among college graduates. (p. 3)

In particular, among people 18 to 44 reading a book not required by school or work fell by 7 percent between 1992 and 2002 (National Endowment for the Arts, 2007, p. 5). This, in effect, refers to reading for "fun," reading for leisure. Whether this reading is popular fiction or fulfilling reading is never specified.

In Canada looking at the average household expenditure on books, there has been a decline from $111 in 2005 to $105 in 2008 (Statistics Canada, 2011, p. 104). Nonetheless:

> Canadians continue to enjoy reading, whether it be newspapers, magazines or books. The GSS [General Social Survey] data reveal that the vast majority of Canadians read for pleasure; moreover, we read quite frequently and devote a substantial amount of our discretionary time to reading. However, fewer of us reported reading in 1998 compared to six years earlier. Eighty-two percent of adult Canadians reported reading newspapers as a form of leisure in 1998, down 10 percentage points from the 92% reporting reading in 1992. A similar drop in readership occurred with respect to magazines. Approximately seven in ten (71%) Canadians reported reading magazines in 1998, a 9 percentage point drop from nearly 80% reading magazines in 1992. Reading books also showed a drop, although less dramatic than that of newspapers or magazines. In 1998, 61% of adult Canadians reported reading books, down 5 percentage points from 1992. (Ogrodnik, 2000, p. 29)

But, since 1998, Canadian magazine and book reading has risen in 2005 to 76.8 percent and 64.9 percent, respectively (Ewoudou, 2005). If the purchase of books is declining, presumably the increased reading of them is to be accounted for by an increased use of libraries, interpersonal borrowing, and online purchases not recorded in the above surveys. Styles (2007, p. 7) writes that in Britain "more people than ever before are reading for pleasure. According to one survey, 65% of people in the UK read for enjoyment compared to 55% in 1979, with a rise in book sales of 19% in five years. Many people prefer to buy rather than borrow their books, although people are using libraries in more ways than ever before."

Reading among contemporary Western adults, as suggested by this limited sample of surveys of their interests, remains reasonably appealing in the smorgasbord of delectable activities that tease the leisure time appetite. Nevertheless, such surveys do not begin to fully examine their reading habits, as established across the immense range of reading material of possible interest to them.

WHAT WE READ

The scope of reading material available to many national populations today is enormous, with none of the sample statistics presented above coming anywhere near covering it. Putting aside for the moment the three broad motives for reading—for utility, pleasure, and fulfillment—the material read enabling their realization comes in four broad types. One is the *periodical*, the magazines, newsletters, newspapers, bulletins, and the like, which may be found online or in hard copy, sometimes both. Most of us, if we read them at all, read selectively certain articles featured within. The second type is that of the *book*, paperback, hardcover, large temporarily bound works (by plastic fasteners, levered clamps, metal rings, etc.), and so on. The OED defines a book as "a collection of sheets of paper or other material, blank, written, or printed, fastened together so as to form a material whole; *esp.* one with sheets pasted or sewn together at the edge, with protective covers."

To this category of reading material, we must add the e-book, downloadable into a computer or an electronic reader like the Kindle.[2] This innovation has ushered in the e-book/printed book controversy. The traditional printed book has its band of avid followers. Rawsthorn (2012) says that they find it well conceived of for the job, being sturdy, light, easy to carry, and, when properly designed, downright beautiful. The e-book apologists hold, in contrast, that theirs is convenient (hundreds of books on a single digital gadget), is environmentally responsible (saves trees), lowers transportation costs, and can be interactive with sound and visuals. Rawsthorn predicts that the printed book, with its superior design, is nonetheless destined to survive, doing so as a relatively expensive niche product falling outside the sphere of popular, pleasurable reading.

de Bury speaks lovingly of print books and how they become closely and emotionally associated with the development of knowledge, pursuit of truth, and experience of personal happiness.

> Moreover, since books are the aptest teachers, as the previous chapter assumes, it is fitting to bestow on them the honour and the affection that we owe to our teachers. In fine, since all men naturally desire to know, and since by means of books we can attain the knowledge of the ancients, which is to be desired beyond all riches, what man living according to nature would not feel the desire of books? And although we know that swine trample pearls under foot, the wise man will not therefore be deterred from gathering the pearls that lie before him. A

library of wisdom, then, is more precious than all wealth, and all things
that are desirable cannot be compared to it. Whoever therefore claims
to be zealous of truth, of happiness, of wisdom or knowledge, aye, even
of the faith, must needs become a lover of books. (de Bury, 1909, pp.
17–18)

What is more, books have their fragrances. British novelist George Robert
Gissing once said that "I know every book of mine by its smell, and I
have but to put my nose between the pages to be reminded of all sorts of
things." Would de Bury and Gissing feel the same about today's e-book?

The third type of reading material is the *pamphlet*, defined in the OED
as "a group of several printed or (formerly) written pages, fewer than
would make a book, fastened together without hard cover and issued in a
single or (formerly) periodical work; *esp.* one of which the text is of a
minor, ephemeral or controversial, nature." Position papers of, say, a
political party or an activist organization often fit this definition, as do
the detailed policy statements occasionally issued by government or by
nonprofit associations. Reports and working papers designed to share
ideas and generate discussion, common in scientific and technical fields,
constitute yet another genre of pamphlet. Brochures, though they may
contain some of what is set out in a larger pamphlet, are too small for our
purposes to be considered reading material.

The fourth type is the *manual*, the conceptual home of an assortment
of practical small volumes: guidebooks, cookbooks, repair and handy-
man books, instructional books, and the like. For some readers textbooks
fall into this set. The object of any manual is to make available helpful
information bearing on how to solve a certain problem, reach a certain
goal, realize a certain project. The sheet or two of instructions on how to
assemble or operate something do not amount to a manual as just defined and, hence, are not reading material as examined in this book.

Cutting points are a problem in this typology, new as it is. For example, when is a book small enough to be thought of as a pamphlet? Perhaps it is less a matter of size than whether there are enough pages to
allow for an enduring binding. We may not be able to judge a book by its
cover, but we may be able to judge whether it is a book by that property.
The cutting point between brochure and pamphlet is also vague. Only
careful research can settle these questions.

The Nature of Reading

These four types of publications contain an array of reading material,
and the motives for reading them can be identified as utilitarian, pleasurable, and fulfilling. The use of manuals is usually driven by utilitarian
interests, though some articles, books, and pamphlets may also be sought
out for this reason. The pleasure found in reading popular fiction usually
comes in book form (including the various kinds of e-books) or it may

occasionally appear as a series of installments in a periodical. The same holds for the belles lettres, literature known for its fine, aesthetic qualities, the reading of which contributes to self-fulfillment. Short stories, whether popular or fine art, may be as short as an article and appear in a periodical. Commercial and fine-arts plays, though meant to be presented on a stage, because they are fiction, may also be read like one would read a novel. Many dramatic texts are book-length. Finally, the essay, usually classified as prose or nonfiction, is a belletristic treatise on a certain subject. It, too, varies considerably in length, running from a work as small as an article to one as large as a good-sized book.

The scholarly scientific (social and physical) and humanistic literature has a home in all this, albeit in a most complex way. The journals in these areas—they are periodicals—provide readers with technical articles, which may be viewed by them as either utilitarian or fulfilling, maybe both. An article that affords a new understanding of a research problem or theoretic puzzle may well be seen by some of its readers as enlightening and hence a vehicle for further personal development. Scholarly monographs and graduate student theses can have the same impact, as can working papers (a kind of pamphlet).

Where does poetry fit in modern reading? Many of the finest poems are short, challenging the principle that reading amounts to an enduring activity, because it takes some time and demands concentration. The justification for including short fine-arts poems in our field of reading material is that, to fully understand them, they must be read slowly and deliberately, possibly several times. Fine-arts poetry, whatever its length, is not doggerel; it is neither trivial nor pedestrian verse.

Where do textbooks fit in this classificatory scheme? It was stated above that textbooks may be classified as manuals, depending on the orientation of their readers. Nonetheless, as will be observed in the next chapter, postsecondary students are, at bottom, serious leisure participants preparing themselves for a career in what they hope will be "devotee work," itself a special kind of serious leisure. Given this orientation, their texts are not manuals, for reading books required as part of a course of instruction in a program they like is fulfilling. And this even while these books survey the area covered, necessarily avoiding a deeper treatment of it and, nowadays, being written for the lowest common denominator of reading proficiency of the targeted audience. Textbooks written for advanced students (upper-level undergraduates and graduate students), though usually also required, discuss the area in greater detail and assume a greater reading proficiency. For people who read texts outside the framework of a course, as part of their own adult or informal continuing education, their goal is even more obviously one of fulfillment. Where textbooks assume a clear utilitarian role is when students must read them in required courses they would rather not take, usually those forced on them by the educational institution in its drive to turn out well-rounded graduates. Mann's (2000) study of university student course reading revealed that, as an activity, they liked their reading in varying degrees, but always with the view of it as problematic, as "work."

WHO READS AND WHY

Official statistics on the reading interests of a population, whether provided by governments or private organizations, never profile those interests in the detail set out in the preceding two sections. Mostly, their data center on reading books in general, with some data focused somewhat more pointedly on reading done for pleasure. It is rare to find information on samples of reading interests focused on manuals, pamphlets, and periodical articles. And reading for utilitarian purposes or for fulfillment is generally ignored in such surveys. Moreover, following Nell (1988, pp. 4–6), some people read for utilitarian, pleasurable, and self-fulfilling reasons, a pattern that further complicates efforts to gain a full understanding of contemporary readership.

These research weaknesses have not, however, prevented some observers from issuing gloomy predictions about the future of reading in the modern Western world, an *aperçu* of which is presented later in this chapter. To be sure, much of today's reading is centered on utilitarian and pleasurable material. The latter will be conceptualized in the next chapter as hedonic, as casual leisure, which nevertheless is not without some redeeming features. The former, meanwhile, as hinted at in the discussion above about students and textbooks, often serves as a powerful resource for finding self-fulfillment and personal development in the serious pursuits (serious leisure and devotee work).

In short, when we regard contemporary reading as a leisure activity in all the complexity of the second, the patterns of reading today and their meaning to readers present a much more optimistic picture than portrayed for us by official statistics. From this angle reading is often a positive experience, however utilitarian, pleasurable, or fulfilling. Erica Jong, an American writer and feminist, once observed: "a book burrows into your life in a very profound way because the experience of reading is not passive" (2003, p. 124).

Reading as Positive Activity

The study of positiveness in the social sciences explores how, when, where, and why people pursue those things in life that they desire, the things they do to create for themselves and (sometimes) society a worthwhile existence that is, in combination, substantially rewarding, satisfying, and fulfilling. I recently set out a positive sociology (Stebbins, 2009a) that joins the somewhat older field of positive psychology in following its interest in uncovering people's strengths and promoting their positive functioning (Snyder and Lopez, 2007, p. 3). As a complement to this branch of psychology, however, positive sociology centers on social meanings, interpersonal interaction, human agency, and the personal and social conditions in which these three unfold with reference to particular human activities. It centers on what people can do and want to do to make their lives worth living, which includes for some of them a fair amount of committed reading.

Reading can be a positive experience, whether that reading be utilitarian, pleasurable, or fulfilling. That said, there are times when we may be drawn or compelled to read about the negative side of life, about one or more of its multitude of problems. Most reading in the social sciences is of this nature, for they have focused and continue to focus on explaining and handling the various problematic, negative aspects of existence that many people dislike, which make their lives disagreeable (see also Jeffries et al., 2006). Controlling or even ameliorating these problems, to the extent this is truly effective, brings welcome relief to those people. Still, managing a community problem in this way, be the problem rampant drug addiction, growing domestic violence, persistent poverty, or enduring labor conflict, is not the same as people pursuing something they like. Instead control of or solutions to these problems bring, in effect, a level of tranquility to life—these efforts make life less disagreeable. This, in turn, gives those who benefit from them some time, energy, and inclination to search for what will now make their existence more agreeable, more worth living, such as by reading a popular novel or a selection of poems written by W. B. Yeats.

Is reading about the negative side of life necessarily a negative experience? Some readers, in their role as citizens, define as an obligation the reading of articles and books about problematic current events and situations. Such reading may be both utilitarian and fulfilling: utilitarian because the material informs the readers about the nature of the problem and its possible solution; fulfilling because it increases their knowledge and understanding of the world in which they live. At the same time such knowledge and understanding can be highly unsettling. Thus, a deeper appreciation of global warming gained by perusing a scientifically credible book on the matter will probably increase the anxiety of people living in areas subject to tornados and hurricanes. In short, reading some material can have both a positive *and* a negative effect on its readers. Moreover, such activity may be understood by them as both a kind of leisure and an instance of nonwork obligation. Here reading spans two of life's three domains.

The Skills of Reading

Francine Prose (2009), in explaining how to be a good writer, empha-sizes the a priori need to be able to read well. She says:

> I read for pleasure, first, but also most analytically, conscious of style, of diction, of how sentences were formed and information was being conveyed, how the writer was structuring a plot, creating characters, employing detail and dialogue. And as I wrote I discovered that writ-ing, like reading, was done one word at a time, one punctuation mark at a time." (locations 86–91, Kindle edition)

Reading in this careful way is accomplished not only word by word, but also sentence by sentence, paragraph by paragraph, and so on as the reader ponders why the writer has chosen the words used, formed the sentences as they appear on the printed page, paragraphed entire pas-sages, and in general structured the text (book, article, poem, etc.) as this person did. Prose also concentrates on the narration of the story, its vari-ous characters, and the dialogue among them. In all this, the committed reader occasionally considers how the text might be improved a bit or at least differently created, as in using alternative words, sentences, para-graphing, narratives, and the like.

There is to be sure more to the skill of reading than this dissecting of text. In novels and short stories there are plots to be analyzed and, if appreciably imaginative, to be admired for their originality. Good writ-ing makes liberal use of alliteration, metaphor, hyperbole, simile, and other figures of speech intended to vividly and imaginatively communi-cate meaning. Careful readers will also notice these creations, marvel if warranted at their effectiveness and imaginativeness, and possibly, as a playful aside, even take a turn at supplying some of their own.

Much of what has just been said also applies to reading skillfully essays, other nonfiction, utilitarian writing, and even some scientific tracts. Here, too, choice of words, structure of sentences, paragraphing, and the layout of the overall work are of utmost importance. There are no plots, but an absorbing use of the figures of speech is always welcome.

Essays and utilitarian texts differ from fictional reading in that they must meet scholarly standards. In other words, there must be adequate evidence for all claims put forth, the logic of the argument must be easily apparent, the work must be grounded in the literature of the relevant fields bearing on the subject of the text, and so on. Skilled readers of such material, using these criteria, will know how to evaluate it.

In sum, the skills of reading fall into two great categories: artistic and analytic. Choice of words, structure of paragraphs, imaginativeness of plot, figures of speech, and so on comprise the artistic side of reading (and writing), whereas readers become analytic when they weigh evi-dence, consider the logic of an argument, and assess how well the work relates to the literature. Utilitarian and fulfilling reading draw on one or both of these sets of skills, while reading for pleasure may be, and indeed often is, done without significant presence of either. This point about pleasurable reading—the hedonic undertaking that it is—will be elaborated in the next chapter under the title of "casual leisure" as well as in chapter 4.

Be aware that committed readers of utilitarian and fulfilling literature are not necessarily, possibly even not usually, competent writers of it. Becoming a competent writer in these two areas rests on, among other conditions, years of experience and practice at the craft. Such people have developed and can now apply the requisite artistic and analytic skills. Given these accomplishments they also know how to read well; they make good readers. This division of expertise is analogous to being, for instance, a competent amateur musician and a knowledgeable hobbyist reader of music history and music theory.

Reading in the Three Domains of Life

Reading is an *activity*, a type of pursuit wherein participants mentally or physically (often both) think or do something, motivated by the hope of achieving a desired end (Stebbins, 2009a). Life is filled with activities, both pleasant and unpleasant: sleeping, mowing the lawn, taking the train to work, having a tooth filled, eating lunch, playing tennis matches, running a meeting, and on and on. Activities, as this list suggests, may be categorized as work, leisure, or nonwork obligation. They are, furthermore, general. In some instances they refer to the behavioral side of recognizable roles, for example, commuter, tennis player, and chair of a meeting. In others we may recognize the activity but not conceive of it so formally as a role, exemplified in someone sleeping, mowing a lawn, or eating lunch (not as patron in a restaurant). A reader in a public library is enacting a role (library patron), but someone reading while sitting on a bench or lying on the grass in a park is engaged in an activity, even while it is not recognizable as a role.

This definition of activity gets further refined in the concept of *core activity*: a distinctive set of interrelated actions or steps that must be followed to achieve the outcome or product that the participant seeks. As with general activities, core activities are pursued in the domains of work, leisure, and nonwork obligation. Consider some examples in serious leisure: a core activity of alpine skiing is descending snow-covered slopes, in cabinet making it is shaping and finishing wood, in volunteer fire fighting it is putting out blazes and rescuing people from them, and in committed reading it is intently consuming printed (or aurally presented) text. In each case the participant takes the interrelated steps necessary to successfully ski downhill, make a cabinet, rescue someone, or peruse the material. In casual leisure, core activities, which are much less complex than in serious leisure, are exemplified in the actions required to hold sociable conversations with friends, savor beautiful scenery, offer simple volunteer services (e.g., handing out leaflets, directing traffic in a theater parking lot, clearing snow off the neighborhood hockey rink), and read entertaining books and articles. Work-related core activities are seen in, for instance, the actions of a surgeon during an operation, the improvisations on a melody by a jazz clarinettist, and the study of professional journal articles. The core activity in mowing a lawn (nonwork obligation) is pushing or riding the mower; in committed reading among university professors it is the requirement of grading term papers, which some define as disagreeable. Executing an attractive core activity and its component steps and actions is a main feature drawing participants to the general activity encompassing it, because this core directly enables them to reach a cherished goal. It is the opposite for disagreeable core activities. In short the core activity has motivational value of its own, even if more strongly held for some activities than others and even if some activities are disagreeable but still have to be done.

At the activity level all of everyday life may be conceptualized as being experienced in one of three domains: leisure, work, and nonwork obligation (Stebbins, 2009a). Reading is no exception. The domain of leisure is the subject of chapter 2, while the other two are covered in this section. Rather little will be said about reading in these initial presentations, leaving to chapters 3 through 5 the task of exploring its complex fit in each domain.

Work

Work, says Herbert Applebaum (1992, p. x), has no satisfactory definition, since the idea relates to all human activities. That caveat aside, he sees work, among other ways, as performance of useful activity (making things, performing services) done as all or part of sustaining life, as a livelihood. Some people are remunerated for their work, whereas others get paid in kind or directly keep body and soul together with the fruits of their labor (e.g., subsistence farming, hunting, fishing). Work, thus defined, is as old as humankind, since all save a few privileged people have always had to ensure their own livelihood. The same may be said for leisure, to the extent that some free time has always existed after work. Today, in the West, most work of the kind considered here is remunerated, but the nonremunerated variety is evident, too. The most celebrated example of the latter is house work, but there are also livelihood-related activities that we tend to conceived of as nonwork obligation (e.g., do-it-yourself home repairs, money-saving dress making). Work, as just defined, is activity people have to do, if they are to meet their economic needs. And though some exceptions are examined later in this section, most people do not particularly like their work. In other words, were their livelihood somehow assured, many of these people would take up more pleasant activities, assuming of course, that they were aware of them and that the activities were accessible.

For many Westerners working time consumes a major part of everyday life, commonly eating up many hours a week from age seventeen or eighteen to sixty-five or seventy and, nowadays, even older. So work is not only a person's livelihood but a major component of his or her lifestyle. But to keep work in perspective, we need to underscore further how much of life for the Westerner is actually not work at all, in that it consists of activity other than that devoted to making a living. In this regard, Applebaum's definition overlooks the fact that making things and performing services can also occur as serious leisure, as any furniture maker or career volunteer, for example, would readily acknowledge.

Moreover, work is not even a universal feature of most Westerners' lifelong existence. First, during childhood and adolescence, most people are not engaged, or are engaged rather little, in work activities. Second, during their working years, some people wind up being unemployed (get fired, laid off, disabled), placing them at least temporarily outside the work force. Third, most people retire, though this status may be blurred because some of them remain partially employed during some or all of this stage of life.

Fourth, even when working full-time in the West as measured by a nation's average work week, workers typically have considerably more nonwork time than work time. Given a full week of 168 hours, an American average work week of 34.8 hours (author calculation from 2005 OECD data reported in *The Economist*, 2006, p. 88), and 70 hours for sleep, and bodily maintenance (including fitness activity), 63.2 hours of nonwork time remain for family, leisure, and nonwork obligations.[3] *The Economist* (2006) also reports that the time working-age Americans, for example, devote to leisure activities has risen by 4 to 8 hours a week over the past 4 decades. This pattern is broken by those who decide (or are forced) to work longer hours or are pressed to put in excessive time meeting nonwork obligations.

Devotee Work

What is critical for the study of leisure in all this is the presence of a small proportion of the working population in the West who find it difficult to separate their work and leisure. These workers, for whom the line between the two domains is blurred, do rely on their work as a livelihood but do this as "occupational devotees" (Stebbins, 2004a). That is, they feel a powerful *occupational devotion*, or strong, positive attachment to a form of self-enhancing work, where the sense of achievement is high and the core activity is endowed with such intense appeal that the line between this work and leisure is virtually erased. Further, it is by way of the core activity of their work that devotees realize a unique combination of, what are for them, strongly seated cultural values (Williams, 2000, p. 146): success, achievement, freedom of action, individual personality, and activity (being involved in something). Other categories of workers may also be animated by some, even all, of these values, but fail for various reasons to realize them in gainful employment.

Occupational devotees turn up chiefly, though not exclusively, in four areas of the economy, providing their work there is, at most, only lightly bureaucratized: certain small businesses, the skilled trades, the consulting and counseling occupations, and the public- and client-centered professions. Public-centered professions are found in the arts, sports, scientific, and entertainment fields, while those that are client-centered abound in such fields as law, teaching, accounting, and medicine (Stebbins, 1992, p. 22). It is assumed in all this that the work and its core activity to which people become devoted carries with it a respectable personal and social identity within their reference groups, since it would be difficult, if not impossible, to be devoted to work that those groups regarded with scorn. Still, positive identification with the job is not a defining condition of occupational devotion, since such identification can develop for other reasons, including high salary, a prestigious employer, and advanced educational qualifications.

The fact of devotee work for some people and its possibility for others signals that work, as one of life's domains, may be highly positive. Granted, most workers are not fortunate enough to find such work. For those who do find it, however, the work meets six criteria (Stebbins, 2004a, p. 9). To generate occupational devotion:

1. The valued core activity must be profound; to perform it acceptability requires substantial skill, knowledge, or experience or a combination of two or three of these.
2. The core must offer significant variety.
3. The core must also offer significant opportunity for creative or innovative work, as a valued expression of individual personality. The adjectives "creative" and "innovative" stress that the undertaking results in something new or different, showing imagination and application of routine skill or knowledge. That is, boredom is likely to develop only after the onset of fatigue experienced from long hours on the job, a point at which significant creativity and innovation are no longer possible.
4. The would-be devotee must have reasonable control over the amount and disposition of time put into the occupation (the value of freedom of action), such that he can prevent it from becoming a burden. Medium and large bureaucracies have tended to subvert this criterion, for, in interest of the survival and development of their organization, managers have felt they must deny their non-

unionized employees this freedom and force them to accept stiff deadlines and heavy workloads. But no activity, be it leisure or work, is so appealing that it invites unlimited participation during all waking hours.

5. The would-be devotee must have both an aptitude and a taste for the work in question. This is, in part, a case of one man's meat being another man's poison. John finds great fulfillment in being a physician, an occupation that holds little appeal for Jane who, instead, adores being a lawyer (work John finds unappealing).

6. The devotees must work in a physical and social milieu that encourages them to pursue often and without significant constraint the core activity. This includes avoidance of excessive paperwork, caseloads, class sizes, market demands, and the like.

This sounds ideal, if not idealistic, but in fact occupations and work roles exist that meet these criteria. These criteria also characterize serious leisure (see Stebbins, 2004a, chap. 4), which gives further substance to the claim being put forward here that such leisure and devotee work occupy a great deal of common ground. When this happens the scope of leisure and the positive lifestyle extend beyond the domain of leisure into that of work, conceptual recognition of which occurs in the next chapter in the idea of "serious pursuit."

Nonwork Obligation

Obligation outside that experienced while pursuing a livelihood is terribly understudied (much of it falls under the heading of family and/or domestic life, while obligatory communal involvements are also possible) and sometimes seriously misunderstood (as in coerced "volunteering"). To speak of obligation is to speak not about how people are prevented from entering certain leisure activities—the object of much of the research on leisure constraints—but about how people fail to define a given activity as leisure or redefine it as other than leisure, as an unpleasant obligation. Obligation is both a state of mind, an attitude—a person feels obligated—and a form of behavior—he must carry out a particular course of action, engage in a particular activity. But even while obligation is substantially mental and behavioral, it roots, too, in the social and cultural world of the obligated actor. Consequently, we may even speak of an overarching culture of obligation that springs up around many work, leisure, and nonwork activities (see Stebbins, 2009a, pp. 53–54).

Obligation fits in the domainal approach in at least two ways: leisure may include certain agreeable obligations and the third domain of life—nonwork obligation—consists of disagreeable requirements capable of undermining positiveness in life in general. *Agreeable obligation* is very much a part of some leisure, evident when such obligation accompanies positive commitment to an activity that evokes pleasant memories and expectations (these two are essential features of leisure; Kaplan, 1960, pp. 22–25). Still, it might be argued that agreeable obligation in leisure is not really felt as obligation, since the participant wants to do the activity anyway. But my research in serious leisure suggests a more complicated picture. My respondents knew that they were supposed to be at a certain place or do a certain thing and knew that they had to make this a priority in their day-to-day living (this exemplifies discretionary time commitment, chap. 6). They not only wanted to do this, they were also required to do it; other activities and demands could wait. At times, the participant's intimates objected to the way he or she prioritized everyday commitments, and this led to friction, creating costs for the first that somewhat diluted the rewards of the leisure in question. Agreeable obligation is also found in devotee work and the other two forms of leisure, though possibly least so in casual leisure.

On the other hand *disagreeable obligation* has no place in leisure, because, among other reasons, it fails to leave the participant with a pleasant memory or expectation of the activity. Rather it is the stuff of the third domain: nonwork obligation. This domain is the classificatory home of all we must do that we would rather avoid that is not related to work (including moonlighting as part of livelihood). These tend to fall into three categories:

Unpaid labor: Activities people do themselves even though they could hire someone else to do them. These activities include mowing the lawn, house work, shovelling the sidewalk, preparing the annual income tax return, do-it-yourself projects, and a myriad of obligations to friends and family (e.g., caring for a sick relative, helping a friend move to another home, arranging a funeral).

Unpleasant tasks: Required activities for which no commercial services exist or, if they exist, most people would avoid using them. Such activities are exemplified in checking in and clearing security at airports, attending a meeting on a community problem, walking the dog each day, driving in city traffic (in this discussion, beyond that related to work), and errands, including routine grocery shopping. Reading lengthy reports fits here, for some people. There are also obligations to family and friends in this type, among them, driving a child to soccer practice and mediating familial quarrels. Many of the "chores" of childhood fall in this category. Finally, activities sometimes mislabeled as volunteering are, in fact, disagreeable obligations from which the individual senses no escape. For example, some parents feel this way about coaching their children's sports teams or helping out with a road trip for the youth orchestra in which their children play.

Self-care: Disagreeable activities designed to maintain or improve in some way the physical or psychological state of the individual. They include getting a haircut, putting on cosmetics, doing health-promoting exercises, going to the dentist, and undergoing a physical examination. Personal and family counseling also fall within this type, as do the activities that accompany getting a divorce.

Some activities in these types are routine obligations, whereas others are only occasional. And, for those who find some significant measure of enjoyment in, say, grocery shopping, preparing the annual income tax return, walking the dog, do-it-yourself projects, or taking physical exercise, these obligations are defined as agreeable; they are effectively leisure. Thus what is disagreeable in the domain of nonwork obligation rests on personal interpretation of the actual or anticipated experience of an activity. So most people dislike or expect to dislike their annual physical examination, but possibly not the hypochondriac.

Nonwork obligation, even if it tends to occupy less time than the other two domains, is not therefore inconsequential. I believe the foregoing types support this observation. Moreover, some of them may be gendered (e.g., housework) and, accordingly, occasional sources of friction and attenuation of positiveness in lifestyle for all concerned. Another leading consequence for positive lifestyle laid down by nonwork obligation is that the second reduces further (after work is done) the amount of free time for leisure and, for some people, devotee work. Such obligation may threaten the latter, because it may reduce the time occupational devotees who, enamored as they are of their core work activities, would like to put in at work as, in effect, overtime.

EXPLAINING THE POPULARITY OF ADULT READING

Adult reading is holding its own among the vast array of activities in the three domains that either demand or invite our time. Part of the explanation for this pattern is economic and geographic and is the subject of this section. Other parts of it are sociological and social psychological. They will be considered in subsequent chapters.

Economics of Adult Reading

First, note that books and periodicals (chiefly magazines and newspapers) are, on the whole, inexpensive compared with many other accessories for leisure and work. True, specialized academic monographs can set back the individual purchaser by well over a hundred dollars (tax and shipping not included), while only institutional libraries can (often reluctantly) afford today's encyclopedias, handbooks, and similar resources. But offsetting these extravagances to some extent are the vibrant used-book businesses, the growing availability of e-books, the practice of borrowing books from libraries or from friends and colleagues, and the paperback market.

Otherwise, magazines and newspapers, being much cheaper to produce than hardcover books, are consequently more affordable, especially if acquired by subscription. Pamphlets are commonly free of charge, often because they carry messages their writers want others to read without being discouraged in this regard by having to pay for them. Manuals usually carry a price tag but often an affordable one. Nonetheless, those who buy them as a means to an end (e.g., travel, legal solutions, do-it-yourself, psychological peace) often face substantial costs once they set about applying what they have learned.

On top of these arrangements are the various book services that sell to subscribers at discounted rates. Book stores have similar arrangements for faithful customers and for special demographic categories known for their low income, among them, retirees, university students, and the unemployed. All this adds up to the conclusion that, often, reading need not be an expensive activity, which appears to be a factor in its continuing appeal in the present depressed economy. For those so inclined they can pursue it as one kind of more or less "nonconsumptive leisure" (Stebbins, 2009b, pp. 118–26).

Geographic Basis of Adult Reading

This section looks at the geographic opportunities for acquiring reading material. The use of public and private space for reading that material will be taken up in chapter 6 under the heading of "reading environments."

When considering the geographic distribution of acquisition points for reading material, what first comes to mind are the bookstores and libraries in town. The former are located where their owners believe they will attract sufficient patrons such as in shopping centers, trendy shopping districts, city centers, and smaller regional commercial centers located in the reasonably moneyed parts of the community. These establishments are situated for easy access by car or mass transit, if not both.

In most medium- and large-sized cities, public libraries are also scattered throughout, with the main and best-stocked of them typically being found in the center. Moreover, if it is older books, periodicals, manuals, and pamphlets that patrons want, especially those out of print, these establishments are the only place to find them. Some university libraries have even greater holdings in these areas, but they are often harder to reach and may exact a substantial fee from external users.

As for periodicals, the most popular of them are available, in addition to the above locations, in kiosks and stalls on busy street corners, public transportation sites (e.g., air terminals, bus depots), convenience stores, supermarkets, and the like. Home or office delivery of subscribed periodicals is also possible. Newspapers may also be available in coin-operated dispensers at bus stops and subway stations. In brief, obtaining such reading is, geographically speaking, little problem for the most part.

We may explain, in part, the modern propensity to read by the easy economic and geographic availability of the most popular and reasonably priced material. Ease of access seems to decrease with the less popular and more expensive material. For example, patrons wanting a new book on a specialized subject in music or painting may have to go to a store that caters exclusively to the needs of musicians or painters or wait for an online order to arrive. The small market for such books (and manuals) keeps their prices high.

MODERN DISTRACTION AND MODERN READING

The alarm has been sounded recently about what Hassan (2012) calls our "high-speed networked economy" and its effects on reading.[4] His alarm is justified on the grounds that electronic connectedness has grown more or less exponentially since 2007, driven by the development of ever more sophisticated devices for sending and receiving messages, like smartphones or tablets. Bosman and Richtel (2012) write that readers of e-books on tablets face continuous distraction from on-screen applications only a touch away. Focusing on reading on these devices, they say, is becoming ever more difficult. All of this is immensely popular with children, adolescents, and adults, but in keeping with the scope of this book, the present discussion will be limited to distraction and reading among the latter.

The distractions made possible by texting, voice phoning, and conversing by way of Facebook and similar services using today's smartphones are very recent and so, therefore, is the sounding of the alarm about these habits and their predicted effects on reading. Hassan (2012, pp. 115–17) offers a good summary of the small but growing literature in the area. He starts with the conclusions of the Pew Internet Project, which inquired into the Internet's future (Anderson and Raine, 2010). This report states that the rate of innovation in electronic gadgets and online applications will continue to accelerate at a remarkable pace, affecting all of society as it gains momentum. The "experts and stakeholders" cited in the report are substantially agreed (76 percent) that this is a favorable trend. Their stance was taken against the backdrop of the much more pessimistic outlook of Carr (2008), who, writing in the *Atlantic Monthly*, maintained that "deep reading" and its companion "deep thinking" can only occur free of distraction, in the quiet spaces and places of daily life. The experts and stakeholders believe, to the contrary, that because of increased availability of information from electronic sources, intelligence will be enhanced. Sixty-five percent of the experts and stakeholders also believed that the "reading, writing, and rendering of knowledge will be improved." A minority of this group believed, however, that by 2020 these three sets of skills will be endangered by the Internet.

Hassan finds Carr's argument compelling, as do I, in part because of a rampant "temporal cognitive dissonance" among many adults defined as a momentary "inability to adequately relate to the meanings of words" (Hassan, 2012, p. 84). Concerning the meanings of words, people suffering from such dissonance fail "either to take their meanings as formal convention would suggest or, more importantly, to think more deeply about the meanings themselves and how they stand the test of being able to satisfactorily describe the functional reality of our lives and the social world more broadly" (p. 84). To a degree previously unknown, people today, whether writing or reading, find themselves unable to properly grasp words except at their most superficial levels. Hassan says this deficiency is rooted in our lack of time. In this conviction he is supported by the earlier ideas of Sabelis (2004).

In fact, when lack of time is introduced into the explanation, it is evident that its effect is more encompassing than temporal cognitive dissonance and a failure to read and think deeply. For without sufficient time readers will be unable to use the reading skills that were described earlier, assuming they have developed them. With a portion of the day taken up texting, twittering, blogging, and generally social networking in cyberspace, the observation that many people have little time for deep reading and thinking about what they read seems plausible.

So what does the evidence say? A recent Nielsen survey indicates that Americans who use the Internet spend an average of 36 percent of their time there "communicating and networking across social networks, blogs, personal e-mail and instant messaging" (Swartz, 2010). Researchers at the comScore Data Mine (2011) found that the average American spends about an hour a day on the Internet. There were variations according to age category, with people in that of forty-five to fifty-four years averaging each month more than thirty-nine hours online.

As a (very) rough calculation it may be hypothesized, given the figures in the preceding paragraph, that the typical American averages around 20 minutes a day engaged in social messaging of some kind. This is not, itself, an outrageous figure, given the 63.2 hours of nonwork time available weekly. Devoting an average of two and one-third hours each week to social messaging still leaves just over 60 hours for other kinds of leisure (and nonwork obligations). Perhaps the issue is not so much the amount of time devoted to electronic distractions but when during the day they occur. Such interruptions at work and leisure, to the extent that the activities being pursued require deep reading and thinking, could certainly disturb concentration for several minutes, possibly longer depending on the message just sent or received.

Not all social communications of the sort considered here are frivolous. A proportion of them may be described as "purposive," as in placing a take-out order at a restaurant, calling parents to let them know of their child's plans and whereabouts, and advising the doctor's office of late arrival for an appointment by a patient tied up in traffic. Purposive messaging may be distracting, but all the same it has become central to the smooth functioning of daily life.

CONCLUSION

The brief sample of data on reading and book-buying habits presented at the beginning of this chapter suggests, on the whole, that adults may be reading as much today as earlier. However, the data suggest that they may be more distracted now and reading, at least some of the time, less effectively than in the days preceding the advent of the high-speed electronic economy. To the extent that the distraction factor is significant, the kind of reading most likely to suffer is that motivated primarily by utility and self-fulfillment. Here concentration is a must. Here the meanings of words may be complex and subtle. Here the reader must often be analytic. In other words, here reading is commonly deep and thoughts about it profound. As for the pleasure-oriented readers they usually escape these exigencies.

The domains of work and leisure, within which all three motivational types of reading take place, form the institutional backdrop for this kind of activity. If we are suffering from a famine of time for deep reading founded significantly on too much social messaging, too many distractions from this area of life, it is in substantial part because of the presence of crucial interests at work or in leisure that also make demands on our time, simultaneously orienting us in their direction. In other words, a noticeable tension has emerged between the kinds of information we seek in the two domains and the ways we seek that information. At issue is the fact that there is from time to time a need for particular kinds of information or knowledge, some of it utilitarian or fulfilling—most of it gained by reading—some of it entertaining or pleasurable—much of it gained these days by social messaging and browsing the Internet. Just how aware we are of this tension is a future research project of appreciable importance. Meanwhile, two fields of scholarship—library and information science and the serious leisure perspective—can shed significant explanatory light on this troublesome feature of modern life and, more generally, on the place of reading there.

NOTES

1. In the United States the Borders chain has closed, while Barnes & Noble is struggling against the same fate, hoping to avoid it, among other ways, with their Nook e-reader (Bosman, 2012a).

2. Reading books on e-readers is relatively uncommon in China, where electronic editions are mostly perused on phones, tablets, and laptops (*The Economist*, 2012a).

3. Some specialists in leisure studies would use "free time" where I have used "nonwork time." My objection to their preference is that some family time and all time spent dealing with other nonwork obligations is anything but free.

4. In fact, this alarm has been sounding for nearly two decades, as evident in Sanders's (1994) call to arms to try to reverse the collapse of writing and reading skills among youth, a process he said was set in motion by the electronic media of the day.

TWO

Leisure and Information in the Study of Reading

Reading furnishes the mind only with materials of knowledge; it is thinking that makes what we read ours.
—John Locke

This book has as its theoretic foundation the serious leisure perspective (SLP) and the framework of library and information science (LIS). Neither covers the full range of reading as an adult activity, for not all reading is leisure and not all reading is motivated by either a desire or a need for information. Be that as it may, the two fields together do constitute a reasonably comprehensive explanation of committed reading as an activity. We turn first to LIS, presenting it only to the extent necessary to integrate it with the SLP in the sections that follow.

READING FOR INFORMATION

Information is knowledge obtained from investigation, study, or instruction as it pertains to a particular subject, event, or other matter of interest and which then may be communicated. Bates (1999, p. 1044) defines the field of library and information science as "the study of the gathering, organizing, storing, retrieving, and dissemination of information." Information seekers "must experience a problem situation," which stimulates them to launch a search for knowledge that will solve the problem (Ross, 1999). In the language of the present book the seeker, in this case the committed reader, needs or desires information to meet a goal, be it utilitarian, pleasurable, or fulfilling. Nonetheless, Ross observes that readers may also serendipitously encounter information and other material that turns out to relate in important ways to their lives. That is, they are sometimes involved in "finding without seeking."

Bates points out that LIS cuts across conventional academic disciplines, as its researchers examine such "processes" as information seeking, teaching, and learning. This is done along lines of various "domains," or universes of recorded information, that are developed and retained for later access. Library and information science is both a pure science and a practical one, with the latter concentrating on the development of services and products for specialties like journalism and library science.

Of the various core concepts in LIS, that of *information behavior* is especially relevant for the SLP and this book. Case (2002, p. 76) observes that this idea captures a range of information-related phenomena, many of which, including serious leisure, have only recently come to the attention of information scientists. He argues that, whereas some researchers conceive of information behavior narrowly in reference only to information-seeking activities, a majority follow Wilson's (1999, p. 249) conceptualization, namely, that information behavior is the "totality of human behavior in relation to the sources and channels of information, including both active and passive information seeking and information use." As Pettigrew, Fidel, and Bruce (2001, p. 44) put it, information behavior centers on "how people need, seek, give, and use information in different contexts."

One of the academic disciplines that LIS has recently come into contact with is that of leisure studies, particularly the SLP. Jenna Hartel pioneered this meeting of the two fields. She pointed out that, historically, LIS has leaned heavily toward studying scholarly and professional informational domains, while largely ignoring those related to leisure (Hartel, 2003). In an attempt to help redress this imbalance, she introduced the study of information in hobbies.

> In some forms of leisure, serious leisure beckons the information behavior community to take leisure seriously, to [use] descriptive and classificatory elements [to] illuminate, isolate, and stabilize serious leisure subjects so that information research can occur rigorously and systematically. This opens an exciting and virtually unexplored frontier for the library and information studies field.

All of serious leisure (to be expanded shortly as "serious pursuits") may be examined for its library and informational forces and properties as these relate to particular core activities and the organizational milieu in which they are pursued. It is known that the patterns of storage, retrieval, and dissemination vary considerably from one core activity to another. Hartel's (2006; 2010) work explored these patterns in the hobby of cooking. Other researchers have examined, for example, information use and dissemination among backpackers (Chang, 2009) and coin collectors (Case, 2009).[1]

Information's Place in Leisure

The concept of information behavior makes a major explanatory contribution to the study of leisure. It does this by centering attention on how participants need, seek (and retrieve), give (disseminate), and use (including storage and organization of) information with reference to different free-time activities and sets of activities (see fig. 2.1). For example, neophytes in golf (beginners in a serious leisure activity) need information on how to improve at the game. They commonly meet this need by seeking utilitarian reading in the form of manuals augmented with personal lessons. They then use this information to work on their game, sometimes telling other neophytes what they have learned. Likewise, someone wanting to make the most of a visit to Italy or learn a foreign language has a need for a certain kind of information, seeks it out, subsequently uses it, and not infrequently tells others about the utility of the information used. Reading a pamphlet, to the extent that this act is agreeable (e.g., a report on the annual evaluation of a nonprofit agency, a written analysis of future directions for a science club), constitutes another instance of information behavior where the information sought is utilitarian. Hartel's hobbyist cooks reported spending countless hours with their cookbooks and related practical resources following, in effect, the model of information behavior.

Beyond these links between information behavior and utilitarian interests lies the complicated role of both in pleasurable reading. Ross (1999) studied how readers use information to choose (i.e., seek) books for enjoyment. She found that her interviewees "usually depended on considerable previous experience and meta-knowledge of authors, publishers, cover art, and conventions for promoting books and sometimes depended on a social network of family or friends who recommended and lent books" (p. 788).

Ross concludes her analysis with five emergent themes bearing on the information search process. One, readers are actively engaged in constructing meaning from their material and applying it to themselves (there is also evidence of this for newspaper readers). Two, the affective dimension is critical to readers' involvement with their material, suggesting that information seeking is sometimes, perhaps often, more than rational problem solving. Thus, reading material may be reassuring, frightening, infuriating, and so forth. Three, readers value the trustworthiness of the recommendations received from others and from impersonal but credible sources of advice on reading (e.g., authoritative book reviews and testimonials). Four, Ross found that reading is framed in a social network of friends and relatives who support a reader's interests and whose interests the reader supports in return. Five, experienced readers choose material using a variety of "clues" about what to look for. These include knowledge about genres, authors, cover art, and the reputation of publishers. Their memory of reviews and advice from friends serve as additional clues. In other words, there is for information behavior an affective/evaluative side as well. That is:

- need for information might rest on love, fear, or pleasure / moral stance (e.g., deviance) or empirical or theoretical requirements;
- information might be sought with intrepidness, anticipation, or curiosity / with a sense of proof or logical fit;
- information might be used with joy, doubt, or excitement/with sense of triumph, accomplishment, or confirmation; and
- information might be given with anger, hesitation, or conviction/ with authoritativeness or impartiality.

Some of these emotions and evaluations are positive, usually part of leisure and the serious pursuits. Others are negative, most commonly being associated with nonwork obligation and disagreeable work.

Ross, in working to extend the conventional lines of inquiry in LIS, and by using pleasurable reading as a vehicle, suggests a number of ways that information both nurtures leisure activities and is nurtured by them. In this regard a main contribution of leisure studies, in general, and the SLP in particular, is the capacity of these two to offer a framework within which to understand the place of information in the lives of individuals and their involvements in the three domains. The intent of the rest of this chapter is to accomplish this framing, albeit primarily for information as it bears on the activity of reading.

THE SERIOUS LEISURE PERSPECTIVE

Before discussing the SLP let us note the definition of leisure on which it is based: *uncoerced, contextually framed activity engaged in during free time, which people want to do and, using their abilities and resources, actually do in either a satisfying or a fulfilling way (or both)* (for a detailed explanation of this definition, see Stebbins, 2012). "Free time" in this definition is time away from unpleasant, or disagreeable, obligation, with pleasant obligation being treated of here as essentially leisure. In other words *homo otiosus*, leisure man, feels no significant coercion to enact the activity in question. Some kinds of work—described in the next section as "devotee work"—can be conceived of as pleasant obligation, in that such workers, though they must make a living performing their work, do this in a highly intrinsically appealing pursuit.

The serious leisure perspective (SLP) can be described, in simplest terms, as the theoretic framework that synthesizes three main forms of leisure showing, at once, their distinctive features, similarities, and inter-relationships (the SLP and its empirical support in research are discussed in detail in Stebbins, 1992; 2001; 2007a). Additionally, the serious leisure perspective considers how the three forms—serious pursuits (serious leisure/devotee work), casual leisure, and project-based leisure—are shaped by various psychological, social, cultural, and historical conditions. Each form serves as a conceptual umbrella for a range of types of related activities. That the SLP takes its name from the first of these should, in no way, suggest that it be regarded, in some abstract sense, as the most important or superior of the three. Rather it is so titled simply because it got its start in the study of serious leisure; such leisure is, strictly from the standpoint of intellectual invention, the godfather of the other two. Furthermore serious leisure has become the bench mark from which analyses of casual and project-based leisure have often been undertaken. So naming the SLP after the first facilitates intellectual recognition; it keeps the idea in familiar territory for all concerned.

My research findings and theoretical musings over the past thirty-nine years have nevertheless evolved and coalesced into a typological map of the world of leisure (for a brief history of the serious leisure perspective, see the history page at www.seriousleisure.net or, for a longer version, see Stebbins, 2007a, chap. 6). That is, so far as known at present, all leisure (at least in Western society) can be classified according to one of the three forms and their several types and subtypes. More precisely the serious leisure perspective offers a classification and explanation of all leisure activities and experiences, as these two are framed in the social psychological, social, cultural, geographical, and historical conditions in which each activity and accompanying experience take place. Figure 2.1 portrays the typological structure of the SLP.

SERIOUS PURSUITS

Devotee work may be conceived of as pleasant obligation, in that such workers, though they must make part or all of their living performing their work, do this in a highly intrinsically appealing pursuit. Work of this sort is essentially serious leisure. In recognition of this sameness, devotee work and serious leisure are now considered under the rubric of the "serious pursuits" (Stebbins, 2012). The present chapter further explains this classificatory change, from what was to this point in the history of the SLP a separation of the two as work and leisure, respectively.

Serious Leisure

Serious leisure, one of the two types of serious pursuit, is the systematic pursuit of an amateur, hobbyist, or volunteer activity sufficiently

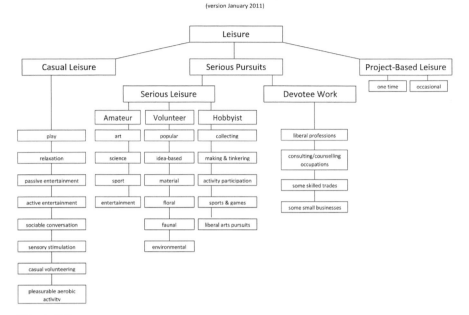

Figure 2.1.

substantial, interesting, and fulfilling for the participant to find a (leisure) career there acquiring and expressing a combination of its special skills, knowledge, and experience. I coined the term (Stebbins, 1982) to express the way the people he interviewed and observed viewed the importance of these three kinds of activity in their everyday lives. The adjective "serious" (a word my research respondents often used) embodies such qualities as earnestness, sincerity, importance, and carefulness, rather than gravity, solemnity, joylessness, distress, and anxiety. Although the second set of terms occasionally describes serious leisure events, they are uncharacteristic of them and fail to nullify or in many cases even dilute the overall fulfillment gained by the participants. The idea of "career" in this definition follows sociological tradition, where careers are seen as available in all substantial, complex roles, including those in leisure. Finally, as we shall see shortly, serious leisure is distinct from casual leisure and project-based leisure.

Amateurs are found in art, science, sport, and entertainment, where they are invariably linked in a variety of ways with professional counterparts. The two can be distinguished descriptively in that the activity in question constitutes a livelihood for professionals but not amateurs. Furthermore, most professionals work full-time at the activity whereas all amateurs pursue it part-time. The part-time professionals in art and entertainment complicate this picture; although they work part-time, their work is judged by other professionals and by the amateurs as of professional quality. Amateurs and professionals are locked in and therefore defined by a system of relations linking them and their publics—the "professional-amateur-public system," or P-A-P system (discussed in more detail in Stebbins, 2007a, pp. 6–8, including Yoder's [1997] addition of the C-PC-AP system). But note here that enactment of the core activity by the professionals in a particular field, to influence amateurs there, must be sufficiently visible to those amateurs. If the amateurs, in general, have no idea of the prowess of their professional counterparts, the latter become irrelevant as role models, and the leisure side of the activity remains at a hobbyist level.

Hobbyists lack this professional alter ego, suggesting that, historically, all amateurs were hobbyists before their fields professionalized. Both types are drawn to their leisure pursuits significantly more by self-interest than by altruism, whereas volunteers engage in activities requiring a more or less equal blend of these two motives. Hobbyists may be classified in five types: collectors, makers and tinkerers, noncompetitive activity participants (e.g., fishing, hiking, orienteering), hobbyist sports and games (e.g., ultimate Frisbee, croquet, gin rummy), and the liberal arts hobbies.

The liberal arts hobbyists—a main consideration in this book (see especially chap. 5)—are enamored of the systematic acquisition of knowledge for its own sake. Many of them accomplish this by reading voraciously in a field of art, sport, cuisine, language, culture, history, science, philosophy, politics, or literature (Stebbins, 1994). But some of them go beyond this to expand their knowledge still further through cultural tourism, documentary videos, television programs, and similar resources. Although the matter has yet to be studied in detail, it is theoretically possible to separate buffs from consumers in the liberal arts hobbies of sport, cuisine, and the fine and entertainment arts. Some people—call them *consumers*—more or less uncritically consume restaurant fare, sports events, or displays of art (concerts, shows, exhibitions) as pure entertainment and sensory stimulation (casual leisure), whereas others—call them *buffs*—participate in these same situations as more or less knowledgeable experts, as serious leisure (for more on this distinction, see Stebbins 2002, chap. 5). The ever rarer Renaissance man of our day may also be classified here, even though such people avoid specializing in one field of learning to acquire, instead, a somewhat more superficial knowledge of a variety of fields. Being broadly well-read is a (liberal arts) hobby of its own.

What have been referred to as "the nature-challenge activities" (Davidson and Stebbins, 2011) fall primarily under the hobbyist heading of noncompetitive, rule-based activity participation. True, actual competitions are sometimes held in, for instance, snowboarding, kayaking, and mountain biking (e.g., fastest time over a particular course), but mostly beating nature is thrill enough. Moreover, other nature hobbies exist, which are also challenging, but in very different ways. Some, most notably fishing and hunting, in essence exploit the natural environment. Still others center on appreciation of the outdoors, among them hiking, backpacking, bird watching, and horseback riding.

Smith, Stebbins, and Dover (2006, pp. 239–40) define *volunteer*—whether economic or volitional—as someone who performs, even for a short period of time, volunteer work in either an informal or a formal setting. It is through volunteer work that this person provides a service or benefit to one or more individuals (they must be outside that person's family), usually receiving no pay, even though people serving in volunteer programs are sometimes compensated for out-of-pocket expenses. Moreover, in the field of nonprofit studies, since no volunteer work is involved, giving (of, say, blood, money, clothing), as an altruistic act, is not considered volunteering. Meanwhile, in the typical case, volunteers who are altruistically providing a service or benefit to others are themselves also benefiting from various rewards experienced during this process (e.g., pleasant social interaction, self-enriching experiences, sense of contributing to nonprofit group success). In other words volunteering is motivated by two basic attitudes: altruism *and* self-interest.

The conception of volunteering that squares best with the idea of leisure revolves, in significant part, around a central subjective motivational question: it must be determined whether volunteers feel they are engaging in an enjoyable (casual leisure), fulfilling (serious leisure), or enjoyable or fulfilling (project-based leisure) core activity that they have had the option to accept or reject on their own terms. A key element in the leisure conception of volunteering is the felt absence of coercion, moral or otherwise, to participate in the volunteer activity (Stebbins, 1996b), an element that, in "marginal volunteering" (Stebbins, 2001b) may be experienced in degrees as more or less coercive. The reigning conception of volunteering in nonprofit sector research is not that of volunteering as leisure but rather volunteering as unpaid work. The first—an *economic* conception—defines volunteering as the absence of payment as livelihood, whether in money or in kind. This definition, for the most part, leaves unanswered the messy question of motivation so crucial to the second, positive sociological, definition, which is a *volitional* conception.

Volitionally speaking, volunteer activities are motivated, in part, by one of six types of interest: interest in activities involving (1) people, (2) ideas, (3) things, (4) flora, (5) fauna, or (6) the natural environment (Stebbins, 2007b). Each type, or combination of types, offers its volunteers an opportunity to pursue, through an altruistic activity, a particular kind of interest. Thus, volunteers interested in working with certain ideas are attracted to idea-based volunteering, while those interested in certain kinds of animals are attracted to faunal volunteering. Interest forms the first dimension of a typology of volunteers and volunteering.

But, since volunteers and volunteering cannot be explained by interest alone, a second dimension is needed. This is supplied by the serious leisure perspective and its three forms. This perspective, as already noted, sets out the motivational and contextual (sociocultural, historical) foundation of the three. The intersections of these two dimensions produce eighteen types of volunteers and volunteering, exemplified in idea-based serious leisure volunteers, material casual leisure volunteering (working with things), and environmental project-based volunteering (see Table 2.1).

Six Qualities

Serious leisure is further defined by six distinctive qualities, qualities uniformly found among its amateurs, hobbyists, and volunteers. One is the occasional need to *persevere*. Participants who want to continue experiencing the same level of fulfillment in the activity have to meet certain challenges from time to time. Thus, musicians must practice assiduously to master difficult musical passages and baseball players must throw repeatedly to perfect favorite pitches. Readers must learn letters, words, and the meanings communicated by words strung together in sentences. Readers must also learn how to read efficiently; that is, they must be able to cover material quickly while grasping its essential meanings. Most difficult is developing a capacity for analyzing what is read (more about this in later chapters). The many skills of reading are well described by Prose (2009). It happens in all three types of serious leisure that deepest fulfillment sometimes comes at the end of the activity rather than during it, from sticking with it through thick and thin, from conquering adversity.

Another quality distinguishing all three types of serious leisure is the opportunity to follow a (leisure) *career* in the endeavor, a career shaped by its own special contingencies, turning points, and stages of achieve-

Table 2.1.   Types of Volunteers and Volunteering

Leisure Interest	Type of Volunteer		
	Serious Leisure (SL)	Casual Leisure (CL)	Project-Based Leisure (PBL)
Popular	SL Popular	CL Popular	PBL Popular
Idea-Based	SL Idea-Based	CL Idea-Based	PBL Idea-Based
Material	SL Material	CL Material	PBL Material
Floral	SL Floral	CL Floral	PBL Floral
Faunal	SL Faunal	CL Faunal	PBL Faunal
Environmental	SL Environmental	CL Environmental	PBL Environmental

ment and involvement. In reading that career consists, in part, of improving as a reader but also consists of an ever-expanding list of materials read. Such a career, in some fields—notably certain arts and sports—may eventually include decline (e.g., a reader's eyesight can seriously deteriorate). Moreover, most, if not all, careers here owe their existence to a third quality: serious leisure participants make significant personal *effort* while using their specially acquired knowledge, training, or skill. In committed reading, effort is required when trying to read efficiently material that is abstract and complex. Reading in a second language may require special effort for those less than fully familiar with it.

Serious leisure is further distinguished by several *durable benefits*: tangible, salutary outcomes such activity for its participants. They include self-actualization, self-enrichment, self-expression, regeneration or renewal of self, feelings of accomplishment, enhancement of self-image, social interaction and sense of belonging, and lasting physical products of the activity (e.g., a painting, scientific paper, piece of furniture). A further benefit—self-gratification, or pure fun, which is by far the most evanescent benefit in this list—is also enjoyed by casual leisure participants. The possibility of realizing such benefits constitutes a powerful goal in serious leisure.

Fifth, serious leisure is distinguished by a unique *ethos* that emerges in parallel with each expression of it. An ethos is the spirit of the community of serious leisure participants, as manifested in shared attitudes, practices, values, beliefs, goals, and so on. The social world of the participants is the organizational milieu in which the associated ethos—at bottom a cultural formation—is expressed (as attitudes, beliefs, values) or realized (as practices, goals). According to Unruh (1979; 1980) every social world has its characteristic groups, events, routines, practices, and organizations. It is held together, to an important degree, by semiformal, or mediated, communication. In other words, in the typical case, social worlds are neither heavily bureaucratized nor substantially organized through intense face-to-face interaction. Rather, communication is commonly mediated by newsletters, posted notices, telephone messages, mass mailings, radio and television announcements, and similar means. Unruh (1980) says of the social world that it

> must be seen as a unit of social organization which is diffuse and amorphous in character. Generally larger than groups or organizations, social worlds are not necessarily defined by formal boundaries, membership lists, or spatial territory. . . . A social world must be seen as an internally recognizable constellation of actors, organizations, events, and practices which have coalesced into a perceived sphere of interest and involvement for participants. Characteristically, a social world lacks a powerful centralized authority structure and is delimited by . . . effective communication and not territory nor formal group membership. (p. 277)

The social world is a diffuse, amorphous entity to be sure, but nevertheless one of great importance in the impersonal, segmented life of the modern urban community. Its importance is further amplified by a parallel element of the special ethos, which is missing from Unruh's conception, namely that such worlds are also constituted of a rich subculture. One function of this subculture is to interrelate the many components of this diffuse and amorphous entity. In other words, there is associated with each social world a set of special norms, values, beliefs, styles, moral principles, performance standards, and similar shared representations. Ross (1999) alluded to the social world of readers in her fourth emergent theme about social networks.

Every social world contains four types of members: strangers, tourists, regulars, and insiders (Unruh, 1979; 1980). The strangers are intermediaries who may participate little in the leisure activity itself, but who nonetheless do something important to make it possible, for example in reading by operating public libraries, publishing books and periodicals, and organizing book fairs. Tourists are temporary participants in a social world; they have come on the scene momentarily for entertainment, diversion, or profit. Most amateur and hobbyist activities have publics of some kind, which are, at bottom, constituted of tourists (we will see in chap. 6 that this type is rare in the reader's social world). The regulars routinely participate in the social world; in serious leisure, they are the amateurs, hobbyists (among them committed readers), and volunteers themselves. The insiders are those among them who show exceptional devotion to the social world they share, to maintaining it and advancing it. Reading insiders include those who, among other achievements, have outstanding reading and analytic skills, have a remarkable record of materials read, and read assiduously and voraciously. The sixth quality—participants in serious leisure tend to identify strongly with their chosen pursuits—springs from the presence of the other five distinctive qualities. Inveterate readers are proud of their commitment to and achievements in the hobby. In contrast most casual leisure, although not usually humiliating or despicable, is nonetheless too fleeting, mundane, and commonplace to become the basis for a distinctive *identity* for most people.

Rewards, Costs, and Motivation

Furthermore certain rewards and costs come with pursuing a hobbyist, amateur, or volunteer activity. Both implicitly and explicitly much of serious leisure theory rests on the following assumption: to understand the meaning of such leisure for those who pursue it is in significant part to understand their motivation for the pursuit. Moreover, one fruitful approach to understanding the motives that lead to serious leisure participation is to study them through the eyes of the participants who, past studies reveal (e.g., Stebbins, 1992, chap. 6; Arai and Pedlar, 1997), see it as a mix of offsetting costs and rewards experienced in the central activity. The rewards of this activity tend to outweigh the costs, however, the result being that the participants usually find a high level of personal fulfilment in them.

In these studies the participant's leisure fulfilment has been found to stem from a constellation of particular rewards gained from the activity, be it boxing, ice climbing, or giving dance lessons to the elderly. Furthermore, the rewards are not only fulfilling in themselves but also fulfilling as counterweights to the costs encountered in the activity. That is, every serious leisure activity contains its own combination of tensions, dislikes, and disappointments that each participant must confront in some way. For instance, an amateur football player may not always like attending daily practices, being bested occasionally by more junior players when there, and being required to sit on the sidelines from time to time while others get experience at his position. Yet he may still regard this activity as highly fulfilling—as (serious) leisure—because it also offers certain powerful rewards.

Put more precisely, then, the drive to find fulfillment in serious leisure is the drive to experience the rewards of a given leisure activity, such that its costs are seen by the participant as more or less insignificant by comparison. This is at once the meaning of the activity for the participant and this person's motivation for engaging in it. It is the motivational sense of the concept of reward that distinguishes it from the idea of durable benefit set out earlier, a concept that, as I said, emphasizes outcomes rather than antecedent conditions. Nonetheless, the two ideas constitute two sides of the same social psychological coin.

The rewards of a serious leisure pursuit are the more or less routine values that attract and hold its enthusiasts. Every serious leisure career both frames and is framed by the continuous search for these rewards, a search that takes months, and in some fields years, before the participant consistently finds deep satisfaction in his or her amateur, hobbyist, or volunteer role.

Ten rewards have so far emerged in the course of the various exploratory studies of amateurs, hobbyists, and career volunteers. As the following list shows, the rewards are predominantly personal.

Personal Rewards

- Personal enrichment (cherished experiences)
- Self-actualization (developing skills, abilities, knowledge)
- Self-expression (expressing skills, abilities, knowledge already developed)
- Self-image (known to others as a particular kind of serious leisure participant)

- Self-gratification (combination of superficial enjoyment and deep fulfillment)
- Re-creation (regeneration) of oneself through serious leisure after a day's work
- Financial return (from a serious leisure activity)

Social Rewards

- Social attraction (associating with other serious leisure participants, with clients as a volunteer, participating in the social world of the activity)
- Group accomplishment (group effort in accomplishing a serious leisure project; senses of helping, being needed, being altruistic)
- Contribution to the maintenance and development of the group (including senses of helping, being needed, being altruistic in making the contribution)

This brief discussion shows that some positive psychological states may be founded, to some extent, on particular negative, often noteworthy, conditions (e.g., tennis elbow, frostbite [cross-country skiing], stage fright, and frustration [in finding time to read, in acquiring certain reading material]). Such conditions can make the senses of achievement and self-fulfillment even more pronounced as the enthusiast manages to conquer adversity. The broader lesson here is that, to understand motivation in serious leisure, we must always examine costs and rewards in their relationship to each other.

Serious leisure experiences also have a negative side. I have always asked my respondents to discuss the costs they face in their serious leisure. It is difficult to develop a general list of them, as has been done for rewards, but in general terms the costs discovered to date may be classified as disappointments, dislikes, or tensions. Nonetheless, all research on serious leisure considered, its costs are not nearly as commonly examined as its rewards, leaving a gap in our understanding that must be filled.

Some rewards may be qualified as thrilling, as sharply exciting events and occasions that stand out in the minds of those who pursue a kind of serious leisure or devotee work. In general, they tend to be associated with the rewards of self-enrichment and, to a lesser extent, those of self-actualization and self-expression. Some rewards are also valued because they include the experience of "flow" (Csikszentmihalyi, 1990). Committed reading appears to generate neither thrills nor flow, a fact discussed in the next chapter.

Costs, Uncontrollability, and Marginality

From the earlier statement about costs and rewards, it is evident why the desire to participate in the core amateur, hobbyist, or volunteer activity can become for some participants some of the time significantly *uncontrollable*. This is because it engenders in its practitioners the desire to engage in the activity beyond the time or the money (if not both) available for it. As a professional violinist once counseled his daughter, "Rachel, never marry an amateur violinist! He will want to play quartets all night" (from Bowen, 1935, p. 93). There seems to be an almost universal desire to upgrade: to own a better set of golf clubs, buy a more powerful telescope, take more dance lessons perhaps from a renowned (and consequently more expensive) professional, read more books or articles, and so forth.

Chances are therefore good that some serious leisure enthusiasts will be eager to spend more time at and money on the core activity than is likely to be countenanced by certain significant others who also make demands on that time and money. The latter may soon come to the interpretation that the enthusiast is more enamored of the core leisure activity than of, say, the partner or spouse. Charges of selfishness may not be long off. Attractive activity and selfishness seem to be natural partners (Stebbins, 2007a, pp. 74–75). Whereas some casual leisure and even project-based leisure can also be uncontrollable, the marginality hypothesis (stated below) implies that such a proclivity is generally significantly stronger among serious leisure participants.

Uncontrollable or not, serious leisure activities, given their intense appeal, can also be viewed as behavioral expressions of the participants' *central life interests* in those activities. In his book by the same title, Robert Dubin (1992) defines this interest as "that portion of a person's total life in which energies are invested in both physical/intellectual activities and in positive emotional states." Sociologically, a central life interest is often associated with a major role in life. And since they can only emerge from positive emotional states, obsessive and compulsive activities can never become central life interests.

Amateurs, and sometimes even the activities they pursue, are marginal in society, for amateurs are neither dabblers (casual leisure) nor professionals (see Stebbins, 2007a, p. 18). Moreover, studies of hobbyists and career volunteers show that they and some of their activities are just as marginal and for many of the same reasons. Several properties of serious leisure give substance to these observations. One, although seemingly illogical according to common sense, is that serious leisure is characterized empirically by an important degree of positive commitment to a pursuit. This commitment is measured, among other ways, by the sizeable investments of time and energy in the leisure made by its devotees and participants. Two, serious leisure is pursued with noticeable intentness, with such passion that Goffman (1963, pp. 144–45) once branded amateurs and hobbyists as the "quietly disaffiliated." People with such orientations toward their leisure are marginal compared with people who go in for the ever-popular forms of much of casual leisure.

Career

Leisure career, introduced earlier as a central component of the defini-tion of serious leisure and as one of its six distinguishing qualities, is important enough as a concept in this exposition of the basics of this form of leisure to warrant still further discussion. One reason for this special treatment is that a person's sense of the unfolding of his or her career in any complex role, leisure roles included, can be a powerful motive to act there. For example, a woman who knits a sweater that a friend praises highly is likely to feel some sense of her own abilities in this hobby and be motivated to continue in it, possibly trying more complicated patterns. Athletes who win awards for excellence in their sport can get from this a similar jolt of enthusiasm for participation there.

Exploratory research on careers in serious leisure has so far proceeded from a broad, rather loose definition: a leisure career is the typical course that carries the amateur, hobbyist, or volunteer through a leisure role and into a work role. The essence of any career, whether in work, leisure, or elsewhere, lies in the temporal continuity of the activities associated with it. Moreover, we are accustomed to thinking of this continuity as one of accumulating rewards and prestige, as progress along these lines from some starting point, even though continuity may also include career retrogression. In the worlds of sport and entertainment, for instance, ath-letes and artists may reach performance peaks early on, after which the prestige and rewards diminish as the limelight shifts to younger, some-times more capable practitioners.

Career continuity may occur predominantly within, between, or out-side organizations. Careers in organizations such as a community orches-tra or hobbyist association only rarely involve the challenge of the "bu-reaucratic crawl," to borrow the imagery of C. Wright Mills. In other words, little or no hierarchy exists for them to climb. Nevertheless, the amateur or hobbyist still gains a profound sense of continuity, and hence career, from his or her more or less steady development as a skilled, experienced, and knowledgeable participant in a particular form of seri-ous leisure and from the deepening fulfillment that accompanies this kind of personal growth. Moreover some volunteer careers may be intra-organizational, a good example of this being available in the world of the barbershop singer (Stebbins, 1996a, chap. 3).

Still, many amateurs and volunteers as well as some hobbyists have careers that bridge two or more organizations. For them, career continu-ity stems from their growing reputations as skilled, knowledgeable prac-titioners and, based on this image, from finding increasingly better lei-sure opportunities available through various outlets (as in different teams, orchestras, organizations, tournaments, exhibitions, journals, con-ferences, contests, shows, and the like). Meanwhile, still other amateurs and hobbyists who pursue noncollective lines of leisure (e.g., tennis, reading, painting, clowning, golf, entertainment magic) are free of even this marginal affiliation with an organization. The extra-organizational career of the informal volunteer, the forever willing and sometimes highly skilled and knowledgeable helper of friends and neighbors, is of this third type.

Serious leisure participants who stick with their activities eventually pass through four, possibly five career stages: beginning, development, establishment, maintenance, and decline. But the boundaries separating these stages are imprecise, for as the condition of continuity suggests, the participant passes largely imperceptibly from one to the next. The beginning lasts as long as is necessary for interest in the activity to take root. Development begins when the interest has taken root and its pursuit becomes more or less routine and systematic. Serious leisure participants advance to the establishment stage once they have moved beyond the requirement of having to learn the basics of their activity. During the maintenance stage, the leisure career is in full bloom; here participants are now able to enjoy to the utmost their pursuit of it, the uncertainties of getting established having been, for the most part, put behind them. By no means all serious leisure participants face decline, but those who do may experience it because of deteriorating mental or physical skills. Occasionally the bloom simply falls off the rose: leisure participants sometimes reach a point of diminishing returns in the activity, having gotten out of it all they believe is available for them. Now it is less fulfilling, perhaps even boring. Now it is time to search for a new activity. A more detailed description of the career framework and its five stages, along with empirical support for them, is available elsewhere (Stebbins, 1992, chap. 5; Heuser, 2005).

The reading career in Western societies commonly begins in early primary school (even earlier in achievement-oriented families), where children learn to read and where some of them develop their initial interest in reading material beyond that required at school. In development, and this may occur later in primary education or at the secondary level, reading certain genres of material becomes routine. By the end of secondary school students are supposed to have acquired the basics of reading as an activity and, with this background, the committed readers among them will have entered the establishment stage. By now these readers will have learned where to find their material, how to pay for it, with whom to discuss it, how to fit it into their lives, and the like. In short, they will have become familiar with and now more or less fully participate in the social world in which their kind of reading is framed. Next, if they continue, they slide gradually and imperceptibly into maintenance, as they become ever more experienced readers, maximizing reading's rewards while minimizing its costs. Decline, if it occurs, may come with seriously weakened eyesight or loss of energy to read with concentration and analytic acumen. The coming chapters will elaborate further the adult stages of the committed reader's career.

Although this can vary according to where in their serious leisure careers participants are, readers can be classified as either *devotees* or *participants*. The devotees are highly dedicated to their pursuits, whereas the participants are only moderately interested in it, albeit significantly more so than dabblers. Participants typically greatly outnumber devotees. Along this dimension devotees and participants are operationally distinguished primarily by the different amounts of time they commit to their hobby, as manifested in engaging in the core activity, training or preparing for it, reading about it, and the like.

This is, however, a rather crude scale of intensity of involvement in a serious leisure activity, a weakness not missed by Siegenthaler and O'Dell (2003, p. 51). Their findings from a study of older golfers and successful aging revealed that data on leisure career are more effectively considered according to three types, labeled by them as "social," "moderate," and "core devotee." The moderate is equivalent to the participant, whereas the social player falls into a class of players who are more skilled and involved than dabblers but less skilled and involved than the moderates (participants). To keep terminology consistent with past theory and research and the generality of the earlier two terms, I have suggested that we calibrate this new, more detailed, involvement scale with appropriate, new terms: *participant, moderate devotee,* and *core devotee* (Stebbins, 2007).

Devotee Work

The subjects of devotee work and occupational devotion have already been discussed in chapter 1 under the heading of the domain of work. What remains to be examined in this chapter is their relationship to reading. Possibly the most obvious affinity between the two is found in the areas of utilitarian and fulfilling reading material. Here professionals and consultants pore over journal articles, research monographs, and pamphlets of various kinds, all in the interest of keeping abreast of the advances in their line of work (utilitarian knowledge) and, simultaneously, maintaining and furthering their expertise (self-fulfillment). Devotees in the trades and small businesses as an adjunct to their work possibly read less literature of this sort. Otherwise, all occupational devotees might also find great satisfaction in reading for leisure outside their work in the various pleasurable and fulfilling genres.

CASUAL LEISURE

Casual leisure is immediately intrinsically rewarding, relatively short-lived pleasurable activity requiring little or no special training to enjoy it.

It is fundamentally hedonic, pursued for its significant level of pure enjoyment, or pleasure. I coined the term in the first conceptual statement
about serious leisure (Stebbins, 1982), which at the time depicted its casual counterpart as all activity not classifiable as serious (nor as project-
based leisure, which I subsequently identified as a third form; see the
next section). Casual leisure is considerably less substantial than serious
leisure, while offering no career of the sort found in the latter.

Its types—there are eight (see fig. 2.1)—include *play* (including dabbling), *relaxation* (e.g., sitting, napping, strolling), *passive entertainment*
(e.g., popular TV, books, recorded music), *active entertainment* (e.g.,
games of chance, party games), *sociable conversation* (e.g., gossiping, jok-
ing, talking about the weather), *sensory stimulation* (e.g., sex, eating,
drinking, sight-seeing), and *casual volunteering* (as opposed to serious leisure, or career, volunteering). Casual volunteering includes handing out
leaflets, stuffing envelopes, and collecting money door-to-door. Note that
dabbling (as play) may occur in the same genre of activity pursued by
amateurs, hobbyists, and career volunteers. The preceding section was
designed, in part, to conceptually separate dabblers from this trio of leisure participants, thereby enabling the reader to interpret with sophisti-
cation references to, for example, "amateurish" activity (e.g., Keen, 2007).

Active entertainment is the conceptual home of pleasurable reading.
Still, it sometimes has a broader reach, in that such material can also
generate a spell of sociable conversation about a book or article of interest
to others in the exchange. And some readers may feel that at least some of
their pleasurable reading promotes relaxation or possibly sparks a bit of
imaginative play.

The last and newest type of casual leisure—*pleasurable aerobic activity*—refers to physical activities that require effort sufficient to cause
marked increase in respiration and heart rate. As applied here the term
"aerobic activity" is broad in scope, encompassing all activity that calls
for such effort, which includes exercise routines pursued collectively in
(narrowly conceived of) aerobics classes and those pursued individually
by way of televised or recorded programs of aerobics (Stebbins, 2004b).
Yet, as with its passive and active cousins in entertainment, pleasurable
aerobic activity is basically casual leisure. That is, to do such activity
requires little more than minimal skill, knowledge, or experience. Examples include the game of the Hash House Harriers (a type of treasure
hunt in the outdoors), kickball, "exergames" for children (videogames
that center on physical activity like dancing; Gerson, 2010), and such
children's pastimes as hide-and-seek.

People seem to pursue the different types of casual leisure in combinations of two and three at least as often as they pursue them separately.
Every type can be relaxing, producing in this fashion play-relaxation,
passive entertainment-relaxation, and so on. Various combinations of
play and sensory stimulation are also possible, as in experimenting, in

deviant or nondeviant ways, with drug use, sexual activity, and thrill seeking through movement. Additionally, sociable conversation accompanies some sessions of sensory stimulation (e.g., recreational drug use, curiosity seeking, displays of beauty) as well as some sessions of relaxation and active and passive entertainment, although such conversation normally tends to be rather truncated in the latter two. Reading, as just depicted, provides still another example.

This brief review of the types of casual leisure reveals that they share at least one central property: all are hedonic. More precisely, all produce a significant level of pure pleasure, or enjoyment, for those participating in them. In broad, colloquial language, casual leisure could serve as the scientific term for the practice of doing what comes naturally. Some of its costs include excessive casual leisure or lack of variety as manifested in boredom or lack of time for leisure activities that contribute to self through acquisition of skills, knowledge, and experience (i.e., serious leisure). Moreover, casual leisure is alone unlikely to produce a distinctive leisure identity. Yet, paradoxically, this leisure is by no means wholly frivolous, for we shall see shortly that some clear benefits come from pursuing it.

It follows that terms such as "pleasure" and "enjoyment" are the more appropriate descriptors of the outcomes of casual leisure in contrast to terms such as "fulfillment" and "reward," which best describe those of serious pursuits. Serious leisure participants interviewed are inclined to describe their involvements as fulfilling or rewarding rather than pleasurable or enjoyable. Still, overlap exists, for both casual and serious leisure offer the hedonic reward of self-gratification (see reward number 5). The activity is fun to do, even if the fun component is considerably more prominent in casual leisure than in its serious counterpart.

For casual leisure, hedonism or self-gratification, although it is a principal reward here, must share the stage with one or two other rewards. Casual leisure, like serious leisure, can also help refresh or regenerate its participants following a lengthy stint of obligatory activity. Furthermore, some forms of casual and serious leisure offer the reward of social attraction, the appeal of being with other people while participating in a common activity. Nevertheless, even though some casual and serious leisure participants share certain rewards, research on this question will likely show that these two types experience them in sharply different ways. For example, the social attraction of belonging to a barbershop chorus or a company of actors with all its specialized shoptalk diverges considerably from that of belonging to a group of people playing a party game or taking a boat tour where such talk is highly unlikely to occur.

Benefits of Casual Leisure

Notwithstanding its hedonic nature, casual leisure is by no means wholly inconsequential; some clear costs and benefits accrue from pursuing it. Moreover, in contrast to the evanescent hedonic property of casual leisure itself, these costs and benefits are enduring. We have so far been able to identify five benefits, or outcomes, of casual leisure, though future research and theorizing may identify others.

One lasting benefit of casual leisure is the creativity and discovery it sometimes engenders. Serendipity, "the quintessential form of informal experimentation, accidental discovery, and spontaneous invention" (Stebbins, 2001c), usually underlies these two processes, suggesting that serendipity and casual leisure are at times closely aligned. In casual leisure, as elsewhere, serendipity can lead to highly varied results, including a new understanding of a home gadget or government policy, a sudden realization that a particular plant or bird exists in the neighborhood, or a different way of making artistic sounds on a musical instrument. We shall see later how reading can engender serendipitous thoughts. Such creativity or discovery is unintended, however, and is therefore accidental. Moreover, it is not ordinarily the result of a problem-solving orientation of people taking part in casual leisure, since most of the time at least, they have little interest in trying to solve problems while engaging in this kind of activity. Usually problems for which solutions must be found emerge at work, while meeting nonwork obligations, or during serious leisure.

Another benefit springs from what has come to be known as *edutainment*, a portmanteau word coined in 1975 by Christopher Daniels (*New World Encyclopedia*, 2008). The term joins education and entertainment in reference to another benefit of casual leisure, one that comes with participating in such mass entertainment as watching films and television programs, listening to popular music, and reading popular books and articles. Theme parks and museums are also considered sources of edutainment. While consuming media or frequenting places of this sort, these participants inadvertently learn something of substance about the social and physical world in which they live. Pleasurable historical novels provide some edutainment for the reading set.

Third, casual leisure affords regeneration, or re-creation, possibly even more so than its counterpart, serious leisure, since the latter can sometimes be intense. Of course, many a leisure studies specialist has observed that leisure in general affords relaxation or entertainment, if not both, and that these constitute two of its principal benefits. What is new, then, in the observation just made is that it distinguishes between casual and serious leisure, and more importantly, that it emphasizes the enduring effects of relaxation and entertainment when they help enhance overall equanimity, most notably in the interstices between periods of intense activity.

A fourth benefit that may flow from participation in casual leisure originates in the development and maintenance of interpersonal relationships. One of its types, the sociable conversation, is particularly fecund in this regard, but other types can also have the same effect. The interpersonal relationships in question are many and varied and encompass those that form between friends, spouses, and members of families. Such relationships, Hutchinson and Kleiber (2005) found in a set of studies of some of the benefits of casual leisure, can foster personal psychological growth by promoting new shared interests and, in the course of this process, new positive appraisals of self.

Well-being is still another benefit that can flow from engaging in casual leisure. Speaking only for the realm of leisure, perhaps the greatest sense of well-being is achieved when a person develops an *optimal leisure lifestyle*. Such a lifestyle is "the deeply satisfying pursuit during free time of one or more substantial, absorbing forms of serious leisure, complemented by a judicious amount of casual leisure" (Stebbins, 2001). People find optimal leisure lifestyles by partaking of leisure activities that individually and in combination realize human potential and enhance quality of life and well-being. Project-based leisure can also enhance a person's leisure lifestyle. A study of kayakers, snowboarders, and mountain and ice climbers (Stebbins, 2005b) revealed that the vast majority of them used various forms of casual leisure to optimally round out their use of free time. For them their serious leisure was a central life interest, but their casual leisure contributed to overall well-being by allowing for relaxation, regeneration, sociability, entertainment, and other activities less intense than their serious leisure.

Still, well-being experienced during free time is more than this, as Hutchinson and Kleiber (2005) observed, since this kind of leisure can contribute to self-protection, as by buffering stress and sustaining coping efforts. Casual leisure can also preserve or restore a sense of self. This was sometimes achieved in their samples, when subjects said they rediscovered in casual leisure fundamental personal or familial values or a view of themselves as caring people. The casual leisure benefits of reading will be explored in chapter 6.

PROJECT-BASED LEISURE

Project-based leisure (Stebbins, 2005a) is the third form of leisure activity and the one most recently added to the serious leisure perspective. It is a short-term, reasonably complicated, one-off or occasional, though infrequent, creative undertaking carried out in free time, or time free of disagreeable obligation. Such leisure requires considerable planning, effort,

and sometimes skill or knowledge, but is for all that neither serious leisure nor intended to develop into such. The adjective "occasional" describes widely spaced undertakings for such regular occasions as religious festivals, someone's birthday, or a national holiday. Volunteering for
a sports event may be seen as an occasional project. The adjective "creative" stresses that the undertaking results in something new or different,
by showing imagination and perhaps routine skill or knowledge. Though
most projects would appear to be continuously pursued until completed,
it is conceivable that some might be interrupted for several weeks,
months, even years (e.g., a stone wall in the back garden that gets finished only after its builder recovers from an operation on his strained
back). Only a rudimentary social world springs up around the project, it
does, in its own particular way, bring together friends, neighbors, or
relatives (e.g., through a genealogical project or Christmas celebrations),
or draw the individual participant into an organizational milieu (e.g.,
through volunteering for a sports event or major convention).

Moreover, it appears that, in some instances, project-based leisure
springs from a sense of obligation to undertake it. If so it is nonetheless
done as leisure, as uncoerced activity, in the sense that the obligation is in
fact "agreeable"—the project creator in executing the project anticipates
finding fulfillment, obligated or not. And worth exploring in future research, given that some obligations can be pleasant and attractive, is the
nature and extent of leisure-like projects carried out within the context of
paid employment. Furthermore, this discussion jibes with the additional
criterion that the project, to qualify as project-based leisure, must be *seen
by the project creator* as a fundamentally uncoerced, fulfilling activity. Finally, note that project-based leisure cannot, by definition, refer to projects executed as part of a person's serious leisure, such as mounting a
star night as an amateur astronomer or a model train display as a collec-
tor.

Though not serious leisure, project-based leisure is enough like it to
justify using the serious leisure perspective to develop a parallel framework for exploring this neglected class of activities. A main difference is
that project-based leisure fails to generate a sense of career. Otherwise,
however, there is the need to persevere, some skill or knowledge may be
required, and, invariably, effort is called for. Also present are recognizable benefits, a special identity, and often a social world of sorts, though
it is usually less complicated than those in which most serious leisure
activities are enacted. Many times the skilled, artistic, or intellectual aspects of the project prove so attractive that the participant decides, after
the fact, to make a leisure career of their pursuit as a hobby or an amateur
activity.

Project-based leisure is also capable of generating many of the rewards experienced in serious leisure. And, as in serious leisure, these
rewards constitute part of the motivational basis for pursuing such high-

ly fulfilling activity. Motivation to undertake a leisure project may have an organizational base, much as many other forms of leisure do (Stebbins, 2002). Small groups, grassroots associations (volunteer groups with few or no paid staff), and volunteer organizations (paid-staff groups using volunteer help) are the most common types of organizations in which people undertake project-based leisure.

Motivationally speaking, project-based leisure may be attractive in substantial part because it, unlike serious leisure, rarely demands long-term commitment. Even occasional projects carry with them the sense that the undertaking in question has a definite end and may even be terminated prematurely. Thus project-based leisure is no central life interest (Dubin, 1992). Rather it is viewed by participants as fulfilling (as distinguished from enjoyable or hedonic) activity that can be experienced comparatively quickly, though certainly not as quickly as casual leisure.

Project-based leisure fits into leisure lifestyle in its own peculiar way as interstitial activity, like some casual leisure but unlike most serious leisure. It can therefore help shape a person's optimal leisure lifestyle. For instance, it can usually be pursued at times convenient for the participant. It follows that project-based leisure is nicely suited to people who, out of proclivity or extensive nonleisure obligations, reject serious leisure and yet have no appetite for a steady diet of casual leisure. Among the candidates for project-based leisure are people with heavy workloads; homemakers, mothers, and fathers with extensive domestic responsibilities; unemployed individuals who, though looking for work, still have time at the moment for (I suspect, mostly one-shot) projects; and avid serious leisure enthusiasts who want a temporary change in their leisure lifestyle. Retired people who often do have time for discretionary activity may find project-based leisure attractive as a way of adding spice and variety to their lifestyles. Beyond these special categories of participant, project-based leisure offers a form of substantial leisure to all adults, adolescents, and even children looking for something interesting and exciting to do in free time that is neither casual nor serious leisure.

Types of Project-Based Leisure

It was noted in the definition just presented that project-based leisure is not all the same. Whereas systematic exploration may reveal others, two types are evident at this time: one-shot projects and occasional projects. These are presented next using the classificatory framework for amateur, hobbyist, and volunteer activities developed earlier in this chapter.

One-Shot Projects

In all these projects people generally use the talents and knowledge they have at hand, even though for some projects they may seek certain instructions beforehand, including reading a book or taking a short course. And some projects resembling hobbyist activity participation may require a modicum of preliminary conditioning. Always, the goal is to undertake successfully the one-off project and nothing more, and sometimes a small amount of background preparation is necessary for this. It is possible that a survey would show that most project-based leisure is hobbyist in character and the next most common is a kind of volunteering. First, the following hobbyist-like projects have so far been identified, with those in the areas of making and tinkering, the liberal arts, and the arts projects often requiring some background utilitarian reading:

- Interlacing, interlocking, and knot-making from kits
- Other kit assembly projects (e.g., stereo tuner, craft store projects)
- Do-it-yourself projects done primarily for fulfillment, some of which may even be undertaken with minimal skill and knowledge (e.g., build a rock wall or a fence, finish a room in the basement, plant a special garden). This could turn into an irregular series of such projects, spread over many years, possibly even transforming the participant into a hobbyist.
- Genealogy (not as ongoing hobby)
- Tourism: special trip, not as part of an extensive personal tour program, to visit different parts of a region, a continent, or much of the world
- Renaissance-man reading projects (e.g., read all the Pulitzer Prize winners in letters and drama for a particular year or set of years)
- preparing for a long back-packing trip, a canoe trip, or a one-off mountain ascent

One-off volunteering projects are also common, though possibly somewhat less so than hobbyist-like projects. And less common than either are the amateur-like projects, which seem to concentrate in the sphere of theater.

- Volunteer at a convention or conference, whether local, national, or international in scope.
- Volunteer at a sporting competition, whether local, national, or international in scope.
- Volunteer at an arts festival or special exhibition mounted in a museum.
- Volunteer to help restore human life or wildlife after a natural or human-made disaster caused by, for instance, a hurricane, earthquake, oil spill, or industrial accident.

- Entertainment theater: produce a skit or one-off community pageant; prepare a home film, video or set of photos.
- Public speaking: prepare a talk for a reunion, an after-dinner speech, an oral position statement on an issue to be discussed at a community meeting.
- Memoirs: therapeutic audio, visual and written productions by the elderly; life histories and autobiographies (all ages); accounts of personal events (all ages) (Stebbins, 2011a).

Occasional Projects

Occasional projects seem more likely to originate in or be motivated by agreeable obligation than their one-off cousins. Examples of occasional projects include the sum of the culinary, decorative, or other creative activities undertaken, for example, at home or at work for a religious occasion or someone's birthday. Likewise, national holidays and similar celebrations sometimes inspire individuals to mount occasional projects consisting of an ensemble of inventive elements.

Unlike one-off projects occasional projects have the potential to become routinized, which happens when new creative possibilities no longer come to mind as the participant arrives at a fulfilling formula wanting no further modification. North Americans who decorate their homes the same way each Christmas season exemplify this situation. Indeed, it can happen that, over the years, such projects may lose their appeal but not their necessity, thereby becoming disagreeable obligations, which their authors no longer define as leisure.

And, lest it be overlooked, note that one-off projects also hold the possibility of becoming unpleasant. Thus, the hobbyist genealogist gets overwhelmed with the details of family history and the challenge of verifying dates. The thought of putting in time and effort doing something once considered leisure but which she now dislikes makes no sense. Likewise, volunteering for a project may turn sour, creating in the volunteer a sense of being faced with a disagreeable obligation that, however, must still be honored. This is leisure no more.

CONCLUSION

Having examined closely both LIS and the SLP, it is perhaps easier now to see how the two complement each other to arrive at a more complete explanation of reading as an activity than is possible using only one of them. The first studies knowledge, the gathering, organizing, storing, retrieving, and dissemination of information, along with the affective/evaluative dimensions of these foci. In general, information is an important part of all three domains of life. In particular, however, it is literally or virtually absent in some activities pursued in leisure and nonwork obligation. Thus, some casual leisure activities, notably play, relaxation, passive entertainment, sociable conversation, and sensory stimulation, seem to require little or no information to engage in them. In the domain of nonwork obligations, mowing the lawn, shovelling the sidewalk, and helping a friend move, for example, also appear to be of this nature. By contrast, all work seems to require information of some kind.

Moreover, in the serious pursuits where all manner of information is needed, organized, and disseminated, the activities people pursue there are further influenced by other important factors. These include their six distinctive qualities, rewards and costs, conditions of uncontrollability and marginality, and the six criteria that distinguish devotee work. Project-based leisure, which is also substantially dependent on information, generates its own set of rewards, while uniquely offering participants a powerfully interesting activity of limited duration. And our nonwork obligations give rise to attitudes that stand apart from the realm of information, including the distaste we have for the core activities themselves, their unwanted tendency to eat away at positive lifestyle, and the inconvenience of such demands.

In sum, to explain more fully an activity like reading, as central as it is to LIS, we must also explore the sociocultural and social psychological contexts in which it is pursued. The "other important factors" mentioned in the preceding paragraph make up major parts of these two contexts. How information in a certain type of leisure is disseminated as reading material and how an emotion like fear or respect can influence the choice of informative reading material are important questions. But answering them still falls far short of being a full explanation of reading.

Nevertheless, the SLP has its own explanatory limits. Most broadly, it cannot be applied in the domains of life filled with disagreeable obligations, notably, nondevotee work and nonwork obligation. Explaining why people engage in activities they dislike falls outside the purview of leisure studies, even while information may well play an important role in those activities. What is more, reading occurs here, most probably the utilitarian variety.

We now move ahead with an LIS/SLP-based elaboration of committed reading. I will not try in this book to carry this elaboration any further, while nevertheless acknowledging that eventually it will be necessary to add a historical component and component on cognitive psychology. Utilitarian reading is the first of the three motivational types to be considered.

NOTE

1. Further theory and research on LIS and the SLP are reported in *Library Trends*, 57, no. 4, 2009.

THREE

Utilitarian Reading

Desultory reading is delightful, but to be beneficial, our reading must
be carefully directed.
—Seneca

Committed utilitarian reading, as opposed to the cursory and detailed
ephemeral types, may be dominantly practical or more or less equally
practical and fulfilling. Utilitarian reading is conducted in all three domains of life: at work, in leisure, and for meeting some nonwork obligations. Moreover, the practical and fulfilling motives for reading are largely carried out in one of three learning contexts: the formal programs
provided by (1) continuing and (2) adult education and the informal
programs and sessions arranged by (3) one or a handful of individuals,
known in leisure studies and allied disciplines as self-directed learning.
Though careful research may demonstrate that utilitarian reading is more
common in adult education and self-directed learning than in continuing
education, there has been to date little scientific study of the matter.
Therefore this observation is best considered hypothetical.

EDUCATION

Reading and oral instruction are two central components of modern education. Education, defined broadly for our purposes, is developing mental or physical powers, sometimes both, as this process leads to formation
of character or an aspect of it. Education of this sort may be formal; it is
given and received in specially designed instructional programs ranging
in length from a few hours (e.g., an adult education course on fly tying) to
many years (e.g., a doctoral program in sociology). Or the education may
be informal, given and received outside such programs by way of advising, mentoring, posing questions, obtaining on-the-job training, coaching

(when not formalized as an organizational program), pursuing self-directed educational activities (e.g., reading, listening, watching), and the like. Nowadays many people use the Internet as a source of informal education, doing this in parallel with the formal courses also available there.[1]

Most educated people appear to develop themselves through formal *and* informal education. Indeed, it is difficult to imagine a kind of devotee work or serious leisure the preparation for which is exclusively formal. Yet there are kinds of work and leisure that some enthusiasts pursue with only informal education, among them, collecting, amateur sport, amateur entertainment, do-it-yourself, and certain small businesses of the devotee variety.[2]

ADULT AND CONTINUING EDUCATION

Since I have examined elsewhere in depth the link between adult education and leisure (Stebbins, 2001a, pp. 94–102), we need only consider it here in broad terms. This will set the stage for a longer discussion on lifelong learning framed in the serious leisure perspective. As a guide I draw on the definition of adult education prepared by UNESCO:

> Adult education is the entire body of organized educational processes, whatever the content, level and method, whether formal or otherwise, whether they prolong or replace initial education in schools, colleges and universities as well as apprenticeship, whereby persons regarded as adult by the society to which they belong develop their abilities, enrich their knowledge, improve their technical or professional qualifications or turn them in a new direction and bring about changes in their attitudes or behavior in the twofold perspective of full personal development and participation in balanced and independent social, economic and cultural development. (UNESCO, 1976, p. 2)

Learning—adult learning in particular—is the object of these educational processes. "Continuing education" sometimes refers to the same processes, although the idea usually connotes extending a person's education beyond the initial education acquired as preparation for a work role (Jarvis, 1995, p. 29).

For the most part, adult education centers on serious rather than casual leisure, though with some of this education also being used to facilitate a leisure project. For instance, amateurs in many arts and scientific fields avail themselves of adult education courses and even whole programs that further their learning of a serious leisure activity. The same may be said for most of the individual amateur sports (e.g., golf, tennis, racquet ball). Still, if we examine all the adult educational programs available in the typical North American city, it becomes clear that they ignore some amateur activities (e.g., handball, rodeo, weight lifting as well as auto and motorcycle racing and virtually all the entertainment arts; Stebbins, 2001a, p. 97).

Adult education, with the exception of collecting, is also a main avenue for learning hobbies. A great range of making and tinkering activities fill the multitude of North American adult education catalogues, including baking, decorating, do-it-yourself projects, raising and breeding, and various crafts (Stebbins, 1998, chap. 3). The same is true for activity participation, which includes such diverse enthusiasms as scuba diving, cross-country skiing, mushroom gathering, and ballroom dancing as well as a few of the hobbyist activities and sports and games (e.g., bridge, orienteering, the martial arts). On the other hand, the liberal arts hobbies are most often acquired purely through self-direction, chiefly by reading. But here, too, we find exceptions, as in the general interest courses offered on certain arts, cultures, philosophies, and histories. Indeed, language instruction is one of the pillars of adult education.

Adult education courses related to volunteerism are mostly offered in such areas as fund raising, accounting and book-keeping as well as management and recruitment of volunteers. To the extent that serious leisure volunteers are involved in these areas, they are apt to be interested in courses bearing on them. Still many career volunteers devote themselves to other tasks, which they learn outside the framework of adult education. That is, the group (club, society, association, organization) in which they serve provides the basic instruction they need to learn further while on the job.

Consonant with Houle's (1961) distinction between learning-oriented and goal-oriented motives for pursuing adult education is the fact that the liberal arts hobbies are the only form of serious leisure where learning is an end in itself. By contrast, for amateurs, volunteers, and other hobbyists, formal educational learning is utilitarian, such as to improve oneself in an art, sport, collecting hobby, or volunteer role of helping others. Thus, some of the students in an adult education course on astronomy will probably be liberal arts hobbyists, while others will be there to learn about the heavens as background for their amateur research. Or the liberal arts hobbyist in, say, French cuisine reads to improve his cultural understanding of this culinary specialty, whereas the cooking (making and tinkering) hobbyist in this area reads to improve her capacity to prepare better gourmet meals. We return to Houle's two motives in the section on self-directed learning.

In all this, reading is usually the main vehicle for learning. Most of what is read is found in a manual, a textbook, or more rarely, journal or magazine articles. Still, some short adult education courses, usually ones centered on activities (e.g., how to wax cross-country skis, read a global positioning system device, find one's way in the night sky using a telescope), may be mostly, if not totally, presented as lectures and demonstrations. This in contrast to the short courses dealing with subjects (e.g., the history of World War II, life of William Shakespeare, birds of western Australia), which are normally based on one or more books. In sum, reading is not an ineluctable part of course-based adult education.

Jones and Symon (2001) draw a similar distinction between adult and continuing education in their exploration of the implications of their differences for governmental policy in Britain. They note that adult education and lifelong learning offer resources oriented toward serious learning for six special groups: the unemployed, unwaged (volunteers), elderly, women, "portfolio workers" (hold many different jobs over a lifetime), and people with disabilities. Serious leisure offers an involving, fulfilling career to these groups that some of their members once had at work and other members never had there. Contemporary governmental policy in Western nations tends to overlook the existence of serious leisure and its implications for personal fulfillment, quality of life, and well-being. Committed reading of all types is among the important serious leisure activities available to these six special groups.

Project-based leisure describes what people are doing when they take one or a few courses, with no intention of further involvement in the subject studied. Many a person has sat through an adult educational course on, say, meteorology, music appreciation, or nineteenth-century philosophy for the pure satisfaction of learning something interesting. Having learned what they set out to learn, they see that "project" as completed, perhaps turning then to a new one.

SELF-DIRECTED LEARNING

Self-directed learning (SDL), sometimes referred to as "autodidacticism," is not limited to reading, even if it is ordinarily a main way of acquiring knowledge in this activity. Such is evident in the definition put forth by Fischer and Scharff (1998), in which they state that SDL is

> a continuous engagement in acquiring, applying and creating knowledge and skills in the context of an individual learner's unique problems. Effectively supporting self-directed learning is one of the critical challenges in supporting lifelong learning. Self-directed learning creates new challenging requirements for learning technologies. Domain-oriented design environments address these challenges by allowing learners to engage in their own problems, by providing contextualized support, and by exploiting breakdowns as opportunities for learning. (from the abstract)

Acquiring and applying skills, as will be noted below, require practice and experience. Where skill is part of the activity about which the participant is reading, the reading itself is insufficient to reach the goals sought.

In fact, in some serious leisure activities, SDL comes mainly by way of observation, possibly accompanied by oral instruction or a training video. Thus, most people learn to play most musical instruments by receiving instruction from a teacher and by watching some demonstrations and performances by the teachers or others.[3] My studies of barbershop singing and Canadian football (Stebbins, 1996a; 1993a) revealed similar kinds of SDL; here reading played a negligible role in learning the activity. In all these pursuits, observation, application, and experience are indispensable ingredients for a successful work or leisure career. Further, success in such fields belies the claim made in the report of the Commission on Reading in the United States (Anderson et al., 1985) that opportunities for personal fulfillment and job success are lost when aspirants to these goals are unable to read.

This brings us to Fischer and Scharff's comment about "domain-oriented design environments," which in the present book are analogous to the serious pursuits. As with these environments each pursuit presents its challenges, is embedded in its own context (e.g., a social world), provides facilitative arrangements (e.g., lessons, practice sites, repair services), and offers opportunities for learning the core activities. Furthermore, the fields of LIS and the SLP, considered together, go well beyond describing these environments to set out the motivational, historical, cultural, and social organizational aspects of the full range of serious pursuits, as these have so far been studied.

Roberson (2005, p. 205), noting the crucial differences between adult education and self-directed learning, links the second to serious leisure. Drawing on an earlier conceptualization by Lambdin (1997), he says that "self-directed learning is intentional and self-planned learning where the individual is clearly in control of this process." Such learning may be formal (here it would be synonymous with adult education), but often it is wholly or partly informal. Agency is an important condition, evident when the learner controls the start, direction, and termination of the learning experience.

Both adult education and self-directed learning are types of *lifelong learning*. The latter (discussed more extensively later) is a broader idea than the first two, summarized by Selman and colleagues (1998, p. 21) as learning done throughout a person's lifetime, "from the cradle to the grave." Furthermore, lifelong learning helps build a *formative career*, or the individual's sense of continuous, positive personal development as it unfolds over the years. It is a subjective concept (Stebbins, 1970), two major components of which are the leisure career and the career in devotee work. Of these two the first is the more foundational, since a large majority of today's devotee occupations actually owe their existence, in one way or another, to one or more serious leisure precursors (Stebbins, 2004a, pp. 73–75).[4]

Roberson (2005) found that his sample of rural, elderly Americans in Georgia took their learning seriously, as they pursued amateur, hobbyist, or volunteer roles. At the same time the respondents also said they "enjoyed" or had "fun" in these learning experiences. Roberson said they were "playful" when involved in them. In fact, his findings would seem to lend some empirical weight to the importance of the serious leisure reward of self-gratification, where participants find a combination of superficial enjoyment and deep self-fulfillment.

For many participants in serious leisure, their SDL can be explained, in part, according to Houle's (1961) distinction between learning-oriented and goal-oriented motives that we considered earlier with reference to education, in general. That is, the liberal arts hobbies are the only form of serious leisure where SDL is achieved primarily by reading and is an end in itself. By contrast, amateurs, volunteers, and other hobbyists read and learn in other ways as means to particular leisure ends, such as producing art, playing sport, collecting objects, or helping others. Sometimes both types of participant enroll in the same adult education course, a pattern that appears to be especially common in science.

As will be observed shortly there are times when people read in preparation for executing a leisure project. Examples abound, as in the leisure-oriented, do-it-yourself enthusiast who pores over a manual on remodeling kitchens, the genealogist who studies the historical literature about the parental old country, and the speaker at a school reunion who, unaccustomed to talking before an audience, examines in advance a pamphlet on public speaking. These examples suggest that SDL in service of projects is largely, if not entirely, goal-oriented, where reading is primarily motivated by practical, utilitarian interests. Indeed, the limited temporal scope of the typical leisure project seems to preclude fulfillment-oriented SDL and related reading, which by dint of being a hobby is a long-term undertaking.

Both of Houle's motives constitute an indispensable orientation toward most complex leisure (especially the serious kind) and devotee work. Such leisure and work require, among other things, that participants learn about the activity, in general, and its core activities, in particular. Thus, learning from one or more sources is unavoidable if a person wants to seriously play the cello, make a quilt, or volunteer to mentor adolescents. All learning here is SDL, in that the participant decides when and where to seek the information and instruction needed to engage effectively in the activity. This would be most difficult to accomplish without the skills of committed reading, with certain exceptions to this observation having been identified earlier in this section.

Application

To the extent that SDL rests on utilitarian-driven reading, it is important to show that this kind of reading does produce practical results. Put otherwise, be it formal or informal, SDL may give the background knowledge needed to pursue a formative career. In some careers of this nature, such knowledge is directly applicable. Thus, the engineer who has learned through readings and lectures how to design a bridge, when called upon to do so, applies what she has been taught. A physician, having learned from books and courses in medical school how to diagnose the common cold, uses that knowledge to treat patients presenting corresponding symptoms. A hobbyist writer, with a course or two on creative writing under his belt, is now ready to apply what he has learned to pen some poems and short stories.

Still, there are occupational devotees and serious leisure participants (amateurs, hobbyists) who must learn further how to use the knowledge they have acquired through reading. For some of these people this entails developing one or more skills, for instance, practicing a golf swing, the musical scales, certain strokes with a calligraphy pen, or the sleight of hand required to execute a magician's trick. Others need a special preparatory learning, as opposed to the background learning acquired through formal and informal education. Preparatory learning is exemplified in learning the lines of a role in a play, the course to be run in a marathon, the responsibilities of a volunteer position, or the rules of contract bridge. In other words, some applications involve no reading at all, whereas others require detailed ephemeral reading before the earlier utilitarian reading can be put to use.

Experience

One of the strengths of the concept of formative career is that it accords a place for experience in the serious pursuits. Gaining experience in such activities takes time; that is, it comes with repeated application of skill, education, and preparatory knowledge. My respondents in the several studies of serious leisure and devotee work that I have conducted over the years (listed in www.seriousleisure.net/bibliography) often talked about the importance of being experienced in what they did. For them greater experience translated into a smoother, less problematic, more efficient pursuit of both the core and the peripheral activities of their work or leisure than was possible with less experience. Put differently, experience elevated still further the positive, worthwhile quality of their participation in these two domains.

But what, in detail, does experience consist of? It consists of familiarity with the usual or typical circumstances and situations in which core activities are pursued, leading to an ever more refined sense of how to pursue those activities. Experience itself is a kind of knowledge, gained as it were on the job and as such differs from the background and preparatory types of knowledge. Some experience results from conscious retrospective observation and reflection (e.g., post-mortem analyses of a concert, game, or speech), whereas other experience is gained subconsciously and expressed in the subtle adjustments seasoned participants automatically make to particular environmental cues. As an example of the latter, I, as a jazz bassist, know from experience when the rhythm section (usually some combination of drums, bass, guitar, and piano) is playing together optimally. My past years in this activity, during which the rhythm has sometimes been optimal and sometimes less so, combine today to tell me how well a given musical group is performing rhythmically or where its problems may lie. Turning to sport, the clever moves of seasoned athletes may be traced, in substantial part, to the subtle lessons of past experience.

Self-directed learning figures in many of the serious pursuits. But, except for the liberal arts hobbies, it is not one of their core activities. We have just seen that SDL is often goal-oriented (i.e., it is often both utilitarian and practical), even while there may be a great deal of it to do. For instance, many a golfer is inclined to read about how to improve at the game as well as how to train for optimal performance at it—two SDL activities—but that person's core activity is actually golfing, including playing on putting greens and driving courses. Note, too, that participants, liberal arts hobbyists included, will find little psychological flow in the SDL undertaken to improve their involvement in complex serious pursuits, even while they will sometimes find it fulfilling (Stebbins, 2010). It is also an indispensable activity in the drive to enhance their work/leisure careers and, more broadly, their lifelong formative careers.

SDL in Society

Self-directed learning is by definition a main vehicle by which personal agency is manifested while pursuing a leisure activity. By engaging in SDL people find maximum freedom to read as they wish, albeit within the usual constraints thrown up by culture, history, and social structure. Such learning obviates the necessity of reporting to someone else, for it is the individual who decides where and how the desired information will be acquired. Still, in the short term, self-directed learners do sometimes have to report to those who evaluate what they have learned, including specialists like instructors, judges, and mentors.

In this fashion SDL can help open the door to possible deviant leisure. It is by way of this process that people discover where their chosen form of deviance or its resources are available for their consumption and use. Examples include gaining information about where a city's strip clubs are located, where clandestine poker games are regularly held (assuming they are illegal), and where and how to buy marijuana on the street. To the extent that reading is involved in these examples, it is of the detailed ephemeral variety. The same holds for people leaning toward anarchism or deviant fundamentalist religion who, wanting contact with kindred spirits, must engage in some discrete reading and inquiring. These latter "seekers" must also learn the fundamentals of these ideological systems.

This, too, is SDL, although in these examples it entails substantial committed reading.

In the past the resources for such learning were typically personal observation and word of mouth and, more formally with some deviance, books, magazines, pamphlets, and the like. Today, these sources are augmented if not supplanted by the Internet. Indeed, the Internet, because of its vast content and obvious convenience, has become arguably the richest repository of all for the kinds of information sought in SDL.

From what has just been said, it may be hypothesized that SDL is fundamental to much of ideational social change. Thus self-directed learning is occurring when people choose to read, listen, or watch a political, religious or other message designed to persuade its audience to think or act differently from the norm. To the extent that they accept what they have learned from such sources, they become part of the anticipated change. Of course, if the message internalized amounts to brainwashing, it cannot be qualified as SDL, since in this instance the self has failed to direct the learning process.

Social change in consumer habits often seems to rest on SDL, as buyers inform themselves through detailed ephemeral reading of the strengths and weaknesses of particular products and services. Some of this kind of change roots in experience with a product or service, this is also SDL, but it is deductive in nature. By contrast, SDL through reading is inherently inductive; information is acquired from existing sources and where appropriate applied to certain problems.

LIFELONG LEARNING

Gallagher (2009) is convinced that our schools all too often kill student interest in lifelong reading and hence in lifelong learning via this route. "To become a lifelong reader, one has to do a lot of varied and interesting reading. If students don't read much at home, school is the only place where 'lighter' reading can take hold. When schools deprive students of the pleasures of recreational reading, we end up graduating test-takers who may never again read for pleasure" (p. 45). This situation among others, Gallagher holds, leads to "readicide." Mann (2000) drew similar conclusions from her study of how first-year undergraduate students approached their required reading. Still, for people who survive this intellectual assault, they live on to savor at some level the faithful companion to lifelong learning: committed reading.

Yet, when we look at adult utilitarian reading as done in continuing education, adult education, and self-directed reading, it is evident that such reading can contribute to an exciting lifelong program. Whether these readers were subjected to readicide has never been studied, but it should be recognized that becoming a utilitarian reader in adulthood is inspired by the characteristic demands of that age, not those of childhood and adolescence. And here, we must remember, utilitarian reading can have both a practical and a self-fulfilling side, as exemplified in scholarly reading and its equivalent outside the academy in industry and government.

Thus, improving oneself in a serious pursuit by reading practical information is often intensely interesting, not to mention powerfully motivating, leading the participant to engage in something predicted to be greatly rewarding. There is the anticipation of getting better at doing what one loves and later the pay off of actually experiencing this improvement. Reading technical information related to a person's devotee work may be dull at times, but it may also be as appealing because it results in self-betterment. Journal articles and research monographs often have a similar magnetic pull on scholars. A practicing youth worker or orthopedic surgeon could well be thrilled after perusing an article to learn of a promising new approach for encouraging adolescents to take up wholesome activities or a more effective procedure for replacing arthritic knees. Exciting lifelong learning may in this regard last for the duration of the participant's involvement in a serious pursuit, notwithstanding the possibility before entering such work or leisure of having experienced readicide in school.

We shall see in chapters 4 and 5 that arrangements like the Book of the Month Club and the formally and informally organized book discussion groups are not usually founded on utilitarian concerns.[5] They are mainly rooted in pleasurable and self-fulfilling interests, and they certainly foster lifelong reading among those members who faithfully peruse the material selected. But, as with these two motivational types, utilitarian readers may well prowl regularly and for many years in bookshops, libraries, and the Internet searching for practical readings related to their work or leisure passion.

LIFE COURSE

Unlike career, linked as it is to particular roles and activities, life course is much broader, covering participation in numerous roles and activities as they evolve, interweave, and are assumed or abandoned across the lifetime of a person (Bush and Simmons, 1981, pp. 155–57).[6] Furthermore, life course, when viewed sociologically, centers on age-graded roles and generational effects. Thus it has a historical dimension in addition to links with social structure based on the status associated with each role and the place of each activity in its domain of work, leisure, or nonwork obligation. For instance, Fisher et al. (1998) observe that old age is uniquely characterized by "generativity," which includes taking on the responsibility of caring for others as realized through such roles as parent, spouse, friend, and grandparent. When not perceived as personal obligation, such care can lead to fulfillment in a leisure role. Of all the age periods composing the life course, the third age, or that period of life between ages fifty and seventy-five (also known as the age of the "young-old" or "active retirement"), offers the richest opportunity for experiencing fulfillment (Laslett, 1994). Brooks (2007) and Wuthnow (2007), by contrast, discuss the little-understood "odyssey years," that period after adolescence and before adulthood (roughly ages eighteen through thirty-five) during which people exist in a state of uncertainty about work, marriage, education, family, and even leisure.

Life course is also broader than the related idea of family life cycle, in that the latter is limited to family matters. Additionally, family life cycle, although chronological as career and life course are, is not essentially processual. Process is a continuous series of actions, events, and changes, and in the social sciences it includes the assumption that these actions emerge from, or are influenced by, each other in seamless fashion. Moreover, this influence may have past (retrospective), present (immediate), and future (prospective) components. Life cycle, on the other hand, deals with historically arrayed, discrete slices of time, often called phases, and within each, events and actions are typically treated of as static. The classic study of leisure and family life cycle is that of Rapoport and Rapoport (1975). In short, life course offers a special slant on leisure and social processes like reading.

Why Is Process Important?

Human social life is, in significant part, processual, and a complete scientific explanation of that life must of necessity include this aspect. Careers and the life course, as processes, are important because they stir up strong motivational forces. Agency is not only a main source of personal action but also the process by which individuals carry out that action. For instance, both success and failure in a career often move them to try to build on the first to achieve still more success and do what they can to avoid the second. Concerning life course people often seem to want, for example, to harmonize personal interests and role obligations. Thus Wearing and Fullagar (1996) concluded from their studies of Australian women that some of them are modifying traditional family roles to put themselves in a position to pursue activities not ordinarily open to females.

Reading interests may vary across the life course in a way that is truly processual. For example, an adolescent girl who loves romantic novels and stories develops during her late twenties an interest in work-related utilitarian literature. Still later she finds that she misses fiction, but now wants something more profound than what she read as a teenager. A friend invites her to join a book club the focus of which is the great literary figures of the country in which they both live. In retirement from the job that required utilitarian reading, she continues with that which retains her interest, making it part of her broader hobby of seeking fulfilment through reading belletristic fiction.

Moreover, both career and life course, by dint of their emergent qualities, encourage people to take stock of what has happened up to a certain point in the unfolding of a particular career or one's entire life. The "life review" (Butler, 1963), said to be common among the elderly, exemplifies stock-taking over nearly all the life course. It involves returning to past experiences and unresolved conflicts to make new interpretations of both, the aim being to reintegrate them into life as it has since unfolded. Successful reintegration can bring new positive significance and meaning to the life course of the subject and prepare this person for death. Likewise, careers in particular roles and activities seem to encourage at numerous junctures both retrospective and prospective reviews of how they have gone and how they will go or may go in the future. Strategizing about how to pursue a career in the present or the future is part of this stock-taking, and to the extent that the observations and possibilities are agreeable, this can be a highly positive process. It can also involve a good deal of fulfilling utilitarian reading, wherein the elderly peruse books and articles written on the meaning of life and their place in it.

This is as true of leisure roles and activities as it is of their nonleisure counterparts. Still, this observation is probably most valid for the serious pursuits, where over the long-term, there are skills and knowledge to develop and apply and experience to accumulate and take advantage of. The life review in old age can certainly include interpretation of the good and the bad experienced in earlier and even ongoing serious pursuits. And pleasurable and fulfilling reading in these areas can augment this review, as when these reviewers study some of the biographies and autobiographies of the greats in their work or leisure passion.

Retirement planning may be similarly viewed. To plan most effectively, workers contemplating retirement must first examine their present work and nonwork lifestyle and then try to forecast with reasonable accurately which aspects of it they would like to continue and which they would like to abandon or change once they have left full-time employment. This includes coming to grips with the nature of the new lifestyle, which could be based on some combination of casual, serious, and project-based leisure, its financial requirements, and the conditions of personal health of self and others on whom the retiree is dependent or who are dependent on the retiree.

A detailed sense of one's past, present, and future needs, interests, and resources is key in effective retirement planning. A survey by Principal Financial Services (2004, p. 4) suggests that as many as half of preretirees have not yet planned for their savings in retirement and only one-fourth have tried to calculate how much they must save for this phase of life. And according to this report they are, during pre-retirement, even less inclined to plan for the leisure facet of their future after work. Here, too, for those so inclined, a veritable library of utilitarian reading on the subject has emerged over the years.

Narrative research offers a fruitful method of data collection on leisure and life course issues. It provides a useful framework for organizing data from narrative interviews that inquire into people's leisure lives. Rich narratives about leisure would seem to be most commonly obtained from enthusiasts who have spent years in a serious leisure activity, who would, it is presumed, have much to recount about their career there and about how that leisure role or activity has meshed with other major roles in their lives. Although not about reading per se, Manning's (1999) work on high-risk narratives gathered from hobbyist adventurers in nature (oceans, jungles, mountains, etc.) illustrates well this approach. And Fullagar and Owler (1998), in a narrative study of people with a mild intellectual disability, were, in effect, looking at life course considerations stemming from their respondents' pursuit of leisure in group settings. The latter qualified such activity as more substantial than the "boring" leisure of entertainment television. Reading groups and clubs number among the interesting alternatives for people with this disability, providing that the material selected is commensurate with their intellectual level.

THE INTERNET AND DIGITAL TECHNOLOGY

The Internet bears on all we have covered so far in this chapter. First, it may be a fount of formal or informal educational knowledge, as seen in (formal) online courses and online encyclopedias and (informal) specialized websites. Put otherwise, the Internet is a tremendous resource for self-directed learning, though users must constantly try to differentiate authoritative from nonauthoritative sources. Second, the Internet is more than a repository of knowledge, since it also the unique venue for certain serious leisure activities, for example, online scrabble, poker, and a tremendous variety of games known only in cyberspace (Silverman, 2006, studied serious leisure participants in massive multiplayer online games). Some online serious leisure activities are fraught with moral implications, however, as in the online hobbyist clubs devoted to revealing the nature of locks and the skills of picking them (Muñoz, 2006) and those that promote mate swapping. Third, the Internet offers information (as distinct from formal education) of practical value in pursuing a career in devotee work or serious leisure. For instance, a professional chemist might go to a website to learn more about a conference he wants to attend. A liberal arts hobbyist might seek books in her area of interest by browsing one or more online book stores. The Internet is a vast wellspring of all three types of reading: committed, cursory, and detailed ephemeral.

The digital world is now also a major arena for both formal and informal education. For instance, databases containing entire digitized books and issues of periodicals are available to subscribers, whether organizations and their members or nonorganized individuals. Some websites have digital libraries stocked with material of interest to registered subscribers or offered free to the interested public. A wide range of material can now be digitized, including written and printed text; drawings, paintings, and photographs; vocal and instrumental music; plans and blueprints; and videos and films. Use of these documents might, for example, be required in completing a formal assignment in a university course or it might be needed in the informal, self-directed educational goal of mastering a serious pursuit at work, in a hobby, or in the world of volunteering.

TRUSTING WHAT WE READ

Of particular importance in any discussion of utilitarian reading is the trustworthiness of the material read. This is not usually an issue in pleasurable reading nor is it in that which is fulfilling, except where the fulfillment is gained from reading utilitarian material.[7] This brings us back to the question of the skills of reading examined in chapter 1. There it was stated with reference to required reading skills that many utilitarian texts differ from fictional reading in that, for these texts to be considered worthwhile, they must meet scholarly standards. That is, they must present adequate evidence for all claims put forth, the logic of the argument must be apparent and sound, the work must be grounded in the literature of the relevant fields bearing on the subject of the text, and so on. Skilled readers of such material, using these criteria, will know how to evaluate it. Then, moving beyond the application of skill and assuming that the material is favorably evaluated, it may be judged as trustworthy. It must not only be properly scholarly, it must also be convincingly reputable.

Readers motivated by utilitarian interests typically confront sets of relevant materials that vary in trustworthiness. Scientific and humanistic researchers whose utilitarian reading appears exclusively in refereed monographs, journal articles, and book chapters, work in an atmosphere of high trustworthiness. By contrast discerning readers will question the trustworthiness of utilitarian material published in the popular literature, in newspapers, magazines, and pamphlets, as well as that found on the Internet.

Partial support for these observations comes from a survey conducted by Leger Marketing for the Association for Canadian Studies. The survey examined Canadians' views of the reliability of information about their country's past, revealing that 84 percent of the respondents judged its museums as the most trustworthy in this area of inquiry (Boswell, 2011). In descending order of reliability after the museums were history books (75.6 percent), direct witnesses of, say, World War II (73 percent), and teachers (71 percent). Only 52 percent of the respondents described on-line sources as very trustworthy. Judgments of trustworthiness of reading material also depend on, in addition to the above-mentioned criteria, reputation of author, sponsor of the material (e.g., a university vs. a manufacturer), modifiability of the material after publication (e.g., open source sites on the Internet), and the like.

This discussion has so far revolved around trustworthiness of scholarly and popular material. Nevertheless, many of the same standards are (or at least should be) applied to reports and guidebooks. For example, I know of no survey data on tourist guidebooks of the sort reported above in the Boswell article. Still, do an Internet search using the phrase "trustworthiness of tourist guidebooks," and you will encounter a multitude of comments on the subject, suggesting that, as a group, they may well evince considerable scientifically verifiable variation along this dimension.

READING AS STUDYING

When we study a written passage or one presented orally that we can rerun, we are in effect rereading that passage. At least three goals are sought in doing this: to understand better the material at hand, ponder its implications, and savor its literary quality. These goals are usually pursued separately, even though two or all three might in principle be pursued simultaneously.

It seems that we reread in all three types of reading. We may need, even in cursory reading, to go over again the timetable of departures for the train, the menu at McDonald's, or the printed directions on how to reach by car a particular business establishment. The need for studying material is, however, much greater when that material is utilitarian. Here even savvy readers must reread certain passages, as they strive to understand them fully and integrate into their own framework of knowledge the ideas being conveyed. Here, too, readers may well want to ruminate on the implications of what they have just learned, doing so by going back over the words before them. At this point the material may spawn new ideas and attendant ramifications. In brief, rereading delivers us from Edmund Burke's warning: "reading without reflecting is like eating without digesting."

Pleasurable and artistically fulfilling reading seem most often to encourage "digestive" rereading aimed at experiencing again the especially captivating way in which a particular passage has been written. Here, following on Burke's metaphor, we might say that the passage tasted so good that the reader wants to swallow another morsel just like it, accomplished through rereading. All three kinds of rereading amount to studying the material at hand, in the sense that readers must again concentrate their minds on it.

UTILITARIAN READING AS OBLIGATION

The place of obligation in work and leisure was examined from a variety angles in the preceding chapter. When it comes to reading as part of meeting an obligation, that reading will most probably be utilitarian. Still, the obligation is not necessarily defined by the participant as disagreeable. Project-based leisure includes many instances of attractive obligatory projects.

A reasonably common North American leisure project requiring some utilitarian reading, while sometimes being defined as attractive, is developing the basement of the family home. For those do-it-yourself enthusiasts who lack practice at this sort of undertaking yet feel the experience will be rewarding (psychologically and economically), they will have to read one or more manuals on the subject. Trustworthiness and cost will probably be among the factors guiding their choice

There will ordinarily be considerable rereading of various passages in these books, as the participant strives to get it right the first time and thereby avoid one possible unpleasant part of the project, namely, undoing and redoing botched steps and procedures. And if all goes well, or as well as might be expected, the material read will probably turn up in conversations about the project held with friends and relatives who have viewed the finished production. Indeed, utilitarian reading often has its social side, as will be made apparent in chapter 6.

Nonetheless, projects can also be disagreeably obligatory—another sour feature of the nonwork obligation domain of life. What is worse under these conditions is that there may be substantial utilitarian reading accompanying them. Such projects are more common than most people would like to think: moving from one residence to another (especially after a long stay in the first place), rehabilitation activities following a major sports injury, serving as executor of an estate, getting a divorce, and on and on. All but the moving example could well involve the obligated person in some substantial utilitarian reading, made that much more unpleasant by having been forced into it as a requirement of the disagreeable project.

Streitfeld (2011) writes about the "do-it-yourself project" of saving one's home from foreclosure. In New Mexico, where affordable legal assistance on this matter is presently difficult to obtain, some homeowners have been driven to try to represent themselves in court. Success in such a project depends significantly on reading and understanding the legal language involved and the procedures for mounting a defence. Here there is plenty of utilitarian reading to do and, in New Mexico, some classes to take at the nonprofit Fair Lending Center. Legal aid groups in other parts of the United States, hobbled by the same shortage of professional manpower, are beginning to offer their own classes on do-it-yourself residential foreclosure.

To this point we have been considering the obligatory reading necessitated by disagreeable projects in the domain of nonwork obligation. Nonetheless, such reading also occasionally darkens life elsewhere, most notably in the domain of work, including even in its devotee wing. The report is arguably the prime exemplar of this kind of unpleasant reading. True, some workers find some reports attractive if they contain interesting information, are decently written, and are not overlong. But other workers—those who view the same reports with a jaundiced eye—look on their executive summaries as a godsend. In addition, workers may from time to time have to learn a new accounting system or other set of administrative procedures, which many feel is an unpleasant, even unwarranted demand on their time. Some of this reading is utilitarian (must digest a small manual), some of it ephemeral and detailed (must digest a few pages of instructions).

Disagreeable reading can upset the lives of devotee workers and, if overabundant, can even force their redefinition of that work as a serious pursuit. This is one concrete expression of the fifth criterion of devotee work set out in chapter 1: the would-be devotee must have both an aptitude and a taste for the work in question. Devotees usually like the reading material that comes with it. Moreover, since they tend to work in minimally bureaucratized conditions, they commonly escape the kinds of utilitarian reading mentioned in the preceding paragraph. Nevertheless, many client-centered professions and small businesses are hedged in by governmental and associational (professional) controls, all of which, when defined by devotee workers as excessive, are capable of weakening the essential leisure heart of their serious pursuit.

CONCLUSION

The popular image of reading tends to be sketched as pleasurable and, in a limited sense, practical and utilitarian. Fulfilling reading—the belles lettres and fulfilling utilitarian reading—are not in the picture seen by the general public. This public seems interested only in the manual side of utilitarian reading (as judged by what is for sale in the standard North American bookstore). Fulfilling utilitarian reading, as served up in scholarly monographs, journal articles, and some textbooks, though recognized as important in the worlds of research and higher education, are virtually unknown beyond it. Meanwhile in scholarly circles the reports, manuals, and ephemeral detailed readings, agreeable or not, have been largely ignored as objects of study.

Images aside, for those contemporary adults who can read at this level, utilitarian reading is sometimes a major part of life. If they are in one of the serious pursuits, it is part of their lifestyle, usually contributing to fulfillment there but sometimes being only an annoying, unavoidable, but nonetheless minor cost (were it a major cost it might justify abandoning the activity). Meanwhile, nondevotee workers and people saddled with disagreeable obligations must cope from time to time with mandatory utilitarian reading they would rather shun.

Thanks to the typology of reading material being explored in this book, we now have some conceptual background with which to design surveys to determine the proportions of a given sample whose reading is motivated by the three types and how often they read along those lines. Such would be necessary should we want a more detailed portrait of reading habits than has been possible up to now. So, to continue our exploration of committed reading in the twenty-first century as undertaken across all three motivational types, we turn next to the most popular of them: pleasurable reading.

NOTES

1. This discussion of education is, for all intents and purposes, about adult, or secondary, socialization. Here the learner, as agent, has a direct and active part in the learning process and in choosing what is to be learned. Not so with much of primary socialization, wherein learning centers on the mandatory acquisition of the basic social and cultural precepts of the society. There is commonly little proactivity possible here.

2. This excludes nonformative careers (defined in note 4) in simple, nondevotee small businesses such as residential garbage collection, hotdog vending, and valet parking service.

3. Instruments like guitar, recorder, and mouth organ are often learned from a pamphlet and, less often, through informal tutelage by a friend or relative.

4. The idea of formative career, during which the person develops in significant measure, must be distinguished from nonformative career, wherein such development is largely absent. Many people have such careers in unskilled work, but movement through them cannot be conceived of as personal development but rather as something else such as accumulated earnings, years of service, and experience with different bosses.

5. Technical professional book clubs do exist, as is evident at BookClubUniverse.com. How popular they are with professionals compared with the level of popularity of the nontechnical clubs remains to be determined.

6. Bush and Simmons do not cover activities. They are my addition done with the intention of harmonizing them with their theoretic presentation in chapter 2.

7. The question of trustworthiness does emerge in pleasurable reading with reference to historical fiction.

FOUR

Reading for Pleasure

Reading, after a certain age, diverts the mind too much from its creative pursuits. Any man who reads too much and uses his own brain too little falls into lazy habits of thinking.
—Albert Einstein

Einstein seems to be castigating all reading, when in fact the utilitarian and fulfilling varieties goad the brain to action. But reading for pleasure—as casual leisure—might have the opposite effect; it is fun and fun might well "use the brain too little." But even casual leisure has its benefits, and pleasurable reading seems not to warrant fully Einstein's blanket condemnation. Before we balance this ledger, let us look more precisely at the ways in which pleasurable reading qualifies as casual leisure, as its own genre of hedonism.

THE PLEASURES OF PLEASURABLE READING

Pleasurable reading is one of the West's most prized hedonic pursuits. On the hedonic theme Lord Chesterfield put it more colorfully: "the mere brute pleasure of reading—the sort of pleasure a cow must have in grazing." It is a type of active entertainment, in that the reader has to concentrate on the words and the story line. Pleasurable reading can also generate a spell of sociable conversation about a book or story of interest to others in the exchange. Moreover, some readers may feel that at least some of their pleasurable reading promotes relaxation or possibly sparks some imaginative play. As Samuel Johnson wrote, "One of the amusements of idleness is reading without the fatigue of attention."

Reading may also provide a kind of sensory stimulation, perhaps most clearly in the case of sexual excitement kindled by erotic, if not pornographic, stories and passages. To be clear, I am not speaking here about visual images but only about printed material. Such literature—romance fiction/erotica—is popular with female readers, who comprise 90 percent of all online consumers of this subgenre (Ogas, 2011). And, now, with e-readers like the Kindle, perusing such material discreetly is becoming increasingly easier (Bosman, 2012b).

Genre fiction in particular provides an array of experiences: casual relaxation, imaginative play, active entertainment, and sensory (i.e., sexual) stimulation. The best of these, as well as more belletristic forms, may be complex enough—demand so high a level of concentration and analysis—as to qualify as fulfilling reading.[1] Additionally, a sociable chat about a given work could conceivably spring from one or more conversationalists who have read in any of the genres classified below (Source: http://www.bsfcs.org/forums/green/Literature/Genres.htm):

All Fiction

Drama: Stories composed in verse or prose, usually for theatrical performance, where conflicts and emotion are expressed through dialogue and action.

Fable: Narration demonstrating a useful truth, especially in which animals speak as humans; legendary, supernatural tale.

Fairy Tale: Story about fairies or other magical creatures, usually for children.

Fantasy: Fiction with strange or other worldly settings or characters; fiction which invites suspension of reality.

Fiction: Narrative literary works whose content is produced by the imagination and is not necessarily based on fact.

Fiction in Verse: Full-length novels with plot, subplot(s), theme(s), major and minor characters, in which the narrative is presented in (usually blank) verse form.

Folklore: The songs, stories, myths, and proverbs of a people or "folk" as handed down by word of mouth.

Historical Fiction: Story with fictional characters and events in a historical setting.

Horror: Fiction in which events evoke a feeling of dread in both the characters and the reader.

Humor: Fiction full of fun, fancy, and excitement, meant to entertain; but can be contained in all genres.

Legend: Story, sometimes of a national or folk hero, which has a basis in fact but also includes imaginative material.

Mystery: Fiction dealing with the solution of a crime or the unraveling of secrets.

Mythology: Legend or traditional narrative, often based in part on historical events, that reveals human behavior and natural phenomena by its symbolism; often pertaining to the actions of the gods.

Poetry: Verse and rhythmic writing with imagery that creates emotional responses.

Realistic Fiction: Story that can actually happen and is true to life.

Science Fiction: Story based on impact of actual, imagined, or potential science, usually set in the future or on other planets.

Short Story: Fiction of such brevity that it supports no subplots.

Tall Tale: Humorous story with blatant exaggerations, swaggering heroes who do the impossible with nonchalance.

All Nonfiction

Biography/Autobiography: Narrative of a person's life, a true story about a real person.

Essay: A short literary composition that reflects the author's outlook or point.

Narrative Nonfiction: Factual information presented in a format which tells a story.

Nonfiction: Informational text dealing with an actual, real-life subject.

Speech: Public address or discourse.

This chapter will not discuss speech as public discourse, it being noted here only because some speeches live on in written form the best of which make for pleasurable reading (e.g., Lincoln's Gettysburg Address, Martin Luther King Jr.'s "I have a Dream," Winston Churchill's "Blood, Sweat, and Tears."[2] But there is little information available about such reading when done as a leisure activity.

READING AS ENTERTAINMENT

One principal meaning of the verb *to entertain* is to provide the public with something enjoyable, or pleasurable, which holds their attention for the period of time the entertaining object or occasion is perceived. In entertainment that truly entertains (recognizing that some would-be entertainment "flops"), attention is diverted from all other matters, hence the occasional usage of one of its synonyms—diversion. In general, these commonsensical terms are employed with reference to what Lewis (1978, pp. 16–17) calls "moderately complex" (as opposed to "simple" or "highly complex") objects and occasions (e.g., a comic strip, television sitcom, popular song, Broadway play, popular novel). Etymologically the verb to entertain evolved from precursors in Latin and Old and Middle French (*entretenir*) meaning to hold.

Of course many things can hold our attention, among them, pain, fear, serious study, and execution of a finely honed skill such as playing the violin, which, in the sense just set out, are anything but entertaining. But when consumers as an audience are truly entertained, they are immersed in one kind of leisure experience. This leisure is primarily pleasurable, one of enjoyment and little else. In a nutshell, it is a type of casual leisure.

Why is reading conceived of as active entertainment? Were reading merely a matter of opening a book cover and "watching" the words inside, we could speak of it as passive entertainment. But reading for pleasure requires concentration, active attention to plot, character, story line, and so on. And there is often no visual material to aid this endeavor, as there is for example in entertainment television. Flights of imagination launched from particular passages of a story are also active responses to the written material. Just how absorbing good pleasurable reading can be is apparent in the following comments by Dominique Browning who found in pleasurable reading the antidote to air-travel-induced boredom. Her comparison of it with fulfilling reading is crisp and trenchant:

> I finally found the literature that stands up to the tests of travel. The secret, dear reader, lies in narrative drive. Plain, old-fashioned, unrelenting, compelling storytelling. You've got to reach for the best-seller shelves. Which, until now, I had avoided with the mild disdain of the librarian who finds herself stamping withdrawal slips for the football team.

> I no longer take Great Literature on the road. It belongs nestled in my arms, deep in a comfortable chair by a crackling fire, where I can tend lovingly to every detail it whispers, where I can pay close attention to the dexterous play of intelligence and the lilting nuance of verbal agility. (Browning, 2012)

How does all this compare with passive entertainment? Here is the classificatory home of sedentary, "couch-potato" leisure that, for its enjoyment, requires little more than turning a dial, pressing a button, flipping a switch, and the like. The passive type an entertainment device—radio, stereo, television set, DVD player—once activated, does all that is necessary to provide the sought after diversion, as provided by one or more entertainers.

Entertainment in Society

An informative theoretic scheme to emerge, in part, from research on entertainment is Lewis's (1978) ideal-typical elaboration of folk, popular, and high culture. Entertainment can be considered part of the second, which includes commercially viable folk music, folk dance, pleasurable reading, and similar arts (indigenous folk culture is essentially noncommercial; see Lewis 1978, p. 16). Two components of these three types are of interest here: (1) structure and appreciation of the form and (2) orientation of the cultural product. In popular culture, the entertaining object or occasion is moderately complex (structure). The highly complex objects and occasions of high culture, which to be appreciated require training, judgment, analysis, and so on, produce experiences for its public that are best qualified as primarily fulfilling (even while pleasure may also be experienced). Another component in Lewis's three types is whether the cultural product is consumer or creator oriented. Entertainment, served up as popular culture, is clearly consumer oriented, unlike the creator-oriented products of high culture.

Is entertainment an art? This is a reasonable question, since the entertaining act or product is simple enough to be understood without significant effort and therefore could conceivably be written off as unartistic. For Munro (1957, p. 45) art includes one or more of three skills:

1. Making or doing something used or intended for use as a stimulus for a satisfactory aesthetic experience. Aspects of this experience may include beauty, pleasantness, interest, and emotion.
2. Expressing and communicating past emotional and other experience, both individual and social
3. Designing, composing, and performing through personal interpretation, as distinguished from routine execution or mechanical reproduction.

Designing and presenting a product that truly entertains a vast public requires all the essential ingredients of art. Thus, although some people providing entertainment do offer their audiences darkly aesthetic or emotionally moving experiences (e.g., soap operas, televised crime shows, romance fiction, murder mysteries), laughter seems to be the main emotion they stir. Most of the time, their role is to amuse. And certainly these artists present something pleasant and interesting. Moreover, there is often considerable personal interpretation inspiring the routining and presentation of an act or the writing of a pleasurable literary work.

But are writers of pleasurable reading "entertainers?" Yes and no. After all, they do not ordinarily perform by presenting pleasurable material to live audiences or remote ones listening or viewing the same material in a television program, video, published photograph, audio recording, or similar media (author readings are an exception). We are accustomed to calling people who do this "entertainers." Still, in the ways just set out, writers of pleasurable literature are entertaining. Cartoonists, comic book writers, most poets and novelists and possibly others entertain with their works, though they do not usually achieve this from a stage. Here lies yet another English-language inconsistency: the process of entertainment is actually broader than the entertainer role, as conceived of in common sense. In other words, pleasurable reading is entertaining, but its authors will not be treated of in this book as entertainers.

READING LAUNCHES IMAGINATIVE PLAY

Casual reading often results in what we may call imaginative play. Nell (1988, p. 206) points out that the play of imagination inspired by reading is an activity apart from reading itself. Simply put, first one must stop looking at the words and then ponder their implications for self or others, if not both. Nell observes that such play may evolve into a "full-blown daydream," during which reading of the inspiring passage temporarily ceases.

Daydreams are complex mental constructions that necessarily take time to work through. Yet, the imaginative play stimulated by reading is not always so involved. For instance, a word might cause us to search momentarily and playfully for a more artistic or precise alternative. A passage might evoke a memory that we now re-imagine in light of the novel and conclude "now I can see that I was wrong" or "that proves that I made the right decision." In such instances, closure on the problematic situation is quickly reached and the reader gets back to the text, possibly with still greater enthusiasm for its content.

Whereas daydreams are commonly conceived of as positive, reading can also evoke negative imaginings. They can be long and nightmarish. Or they may be short and practical: that passage suggests that I'd better check on how well my own home is covered by fire insurance or that I'd better be sure to lock the doors of my car while driving it. Ironically, pleasurable reading is done for enjoyment, even though it does not always spawn pure joy.

Literary metaphors can also open the door to imaginative play. Shakespeare's celebrated metaphor "all the world's a stage" could easily set readers to thinking about how they are enacting their own roles in life, "their exits and their entrances." Or as P. J. O'Rourke wrote: "giving money and power to government is like giving whiskey and car keys to teenage boys." Having read this rant the reader might be inclined to ruminate about the recklessness and irresponsibility of government, examples of which are legion these days.[3] Markus Zusak wrote in *I Am The Messenger*: "A dark wind makes it through the trees. The sky is nervous. Black and blue." Such a passage offers a vivid invitation to think about some of the foreboding meteorological conditions that the reader has directly experienced, perhaps gingered up with memories of their unsettling consequences and possibilities.

Now the modern age has handed our imagination a new tool: Amazon's Kindle Store is now selling Coliloquy e-books in which scattered "choice points" appear. These junctures enable readers to rewrite the story in their own terms, according to their imaginative desires, say, with a different character, same character with some traits modified, or different key background conditions. The books come with active applications capable of accepting such changes and even allowing readers to update the material. With Coliloquy's romance fiction (classified here as realistic fiction), these innovations could lead to some do-it-yourself soap opera.

Jasper Fforde, in *The Well of Lost Plots*, sums up this section well: "after all, reading is arguably a far more creative and imaginative process than writing; when the reader creates emotion in their head, or the colors of the sky during the setting sun, or the smell of a warm summer's breeze on their face, they should reserve as much praise for themselves as they do for the writer—perhaps more." Nevertheless, reading cannot foster imaginative play at every word, for if it did, we would be forever trying to finish the book at hand. At work against stopping incessantly to lapse into reverie or follow through with metaphors is the desire to move forward in the plot. Too many playful side trips may cause the reader to lose his way in the text.

READING LEADS TO SOCIABLE CONVERSATION

According to Simmel (1949), the essence of sociable conversation lies in its playfulness, a quality enjoyed for its intrinsic value. Sociable conversation guarantees the participants maximization of such values as joy, relief, and vivacity; it is democratic activity in that the pleasure of one person is dependent on that of the other people in the exchange. Because it is noninstrumental interaction between individuals, sociable conversation is destroyed when someone introduces a wholly personal interest or goal and is maintained when all participants exhibit amiability, cordiality, attractiveness, and proper breeding.

Sociable conversations can spring up in a wide variety of settings. They may develop in such public conveyances as buses, taxis, and airplanes. Waiting rooms and bus stops may give rise to sociable conversations among those with no choice but to be there. Perhaps the most common platforms for conversation are planned events like receptions, private parties, and after-hours gatherings. Of course, to the extent that these get-togethers become instrumental, or problem-centered, as they can when work or some other obligation insinuates itself, their leisure character fades in proportion.

Reading material can became the object of conversation anywhere, but it is most commonly at book clubs.[4] Book clubs can meet in libraries, bookstores, cafes, or private homes. In large cities, book clubs that are open to the public list their meeting dates and current picks in newspapers and online. Book clubs can even be centered on a TV show, as in the case of Oprah Winfrey's book club, which has attracted thousands of isolated readers to share their thoughts about volumes she identified as worthy of such attention. Moreover, though pleasurable reading is not normally the object of interest, professional organizations often have associated reading groups or their equivalent. For example, the American

Sociological Association holds at each annual conference a number of sessions entitled "Author Meets Critics," wherein a single book is targeted for comment first by an invited panel and then by the larger audience attending the event.

Online book clubs exist as well. Websites like bookclubsonline.org, book-club-resource.com, and goodreads.com provide commentary from readers, help individuals start or join a book club, and maintain chat rooms and author interviews. The latest wrinkle in e-reading is "social reading": texted communication using an e-reading device like the Kindle or an iPad to discuss with other people the text you are perusing (Kellogg, 2012). Using special applications it is possible to simultaneously involve several people in the conversation, all of whom can also view the same printed material. For one application there is talk of bringing an entire book club into a mass, on-the-spot exchange animated by an interesting passage.

READING AS SENSORY STIMULATION

Pleasurable reading generally provides positive, agreeable stimulation through the eyes and, for those with visual problems, through the ears when the written material is read to them and the fingers when Braille is the means of communication. What sort of sensory charge can people get from reading, feeling, or hearing pleasurable written material?

The sensory charge gained from reading can be immense, though only if the material is written well. The underlying mechanism at work here is that words can evoke arousing images and personal memories. The content of these images and memories can have a wide variety of effects—sexual, aesthetic, fantastic (escapist), compassionate, frightful, and so on. This is, of course, what authors intend, although there may occur for certain readers some idiosyncratic imagery or memories that are unexpected, perhaps even regretted. Thus, a novelist using some well-chosen words intends to generate fright in the novel's readers, but a few of them experience pride instead, as they imagine themselves as champions of good over the evil fearsome situation. The author might regret that a few readers have nightmares from the passage in question, the intention not being to upset anyone to that extent.

Another type of sensory stimulation is pleasure from the words themselves. Alta Language Services (2009), one function of which is translation, has set about identifying some of the most beautiful words in the English language. Alta argues that "A unique combination of vowel and consonant sounds, coupled with a nuanced or associative meaning of a word, can create an aesthetically satisfying phonologic harmony and musicality." Based on data gathered from surveys, they suggest that anglophones tend to favor words featuring "S" and "Q" sounds, with the musicality of a word being more important than its associative meaning. Among the words it lists that possess this quality are bubble, perspicacious, diaphanous, susurrus, ephemeral, and arboreal. A number of loan words from Dutch, French, German, and Russian, among other languages, were also highly rated in Alta's linguistic beauty contest.

We see and hear this beauty, but do we feel it when touching Braille letters? Possibly, in that the aesthetic side of words lies in their musicality, which we hear and which blind people could also hear prior to their contact with the Braille presentation of the word in question. That is, when we read "perspicacious" we sense its pronunciation and may even utter it *sotto voce* to ourselves. A blind person, having heard people say that word and possibly even having used it, could also sense its pronunciation when the word comes up in Braille.

There are also ugly-sounding words; they stimulate the sensations of disgust or revulsion. Alta Language Services (2010) also has a list of these sensory offenders as identified through online surveys. They include phlegm, pus, pregnant, rural, moist, juror, and regurgitate. Associative meaning appears to play a more central role here than in the beautiful words above. Some ugly words also roll clumsily off the tongue: phlegm, sticktoitiveness, ointment, and crepuscular being prime examples. Again, with such words, the a priori act of pronunciation helps create a feeling of revulsion.

Since all leisure is essentially positive—most obviously so in the casual form—ugly words and their sensory concomitants encountered during pleasurable reading are, in theory, rather unseemly. Some authors, as part of their broader design of plot and story line, may intentionally jar their readers with such words; others undermine their writing's beauty unintentionally.

Hearing written material, as in public author readings and private readings to children and people whose handicaps preclude reading on their own, adds yet another dimension to the sensation of reading. That dimension is theatrical. In face-to-face situations the presenter of the material can act out in speech and gesture the text being read aloud. The arts of writing and drama are hereby joined to deliver an even greater jolt of pleasure gained from pleasurable reading (an exceptional instance being the reading onstage of *Peter and the Wolf*, enhanced appreciably by Prokofiev's wonderful musical background). The gestural component is lost when the listener (reader) hears written material by way of an audio CD, radio broadcast, audio tape, telephone conversation, and the like.[5] Nonetheless, the aural part remains, and surely there is considerable added value for the listener-reader in consuming pleasurable material this way.

READING AS RELAXATION

To relax is to reduce either the psychological or the physical tension from which one is suffering. Most relaxation—perhaps its most effective manifestations—includes both of these. Reading can be relaxing, but still not all reading nurtures this state under all conditions.

The material most likely to relax readers is the pleasurable kind. Utilitarian and fulfilling reading—requiring as they do concentration, analysis, cogitation, synthesis, and other mental activities—are less than wholly relaxing. Readers may be comfortably seated for pursuing this more demanding undertaking, but their minds are active at the high level needed to gain the sought after utility or fulfillment (see the Browning quotation above). Pleasurable readers also tend to be physically relaxed, while being absorbed in reading material that facilitates their mental relaxation as well.

It is getting pulled into the story that brings about relaxation through pleasurable reading. Nell (1988, p. 209) supports this causal link with his conclusions about Eric Klinger's work on fantasy: "A single startling insight thus explains one of ludic [pleasurable] reading's greatest attractions, its effortlessness." Put otherwise, the story's magnetic appeal obviates any need to make an effort to continue reading, with the result that the reader experiences a release of tension as time passes, book in hand.

Radway (1999) reports on her struggle as a graduate student in English to embrace with the same degree of enthusiasm the high-culture literature of her academic studies that she had for the popular-culture, pleasurable reading she learned to love during her childhood.

> But that appreciation, no matter how intense, was always combined with an intellectual distance connected to the manner in which I had acquired this new competence, that is, in school classrooms and under the sway of authoritative experts. As a consequence my new tastes somehow failed to duplicate precisely the passion of my response to those other, suspect, supposedly transparent, popular books. Those books prompted physical sensations, a forgetting of the self and complete absorption in another world. The books that came to me as high culture never seemed to prompt the particular shudder, the frisson I associated with the books of my childhood. (p. 3)

Relaxation, while being one type of casual leisure, is also a component of some of the other types of such leisure. When in common sense we think of leisure in general, we think of relaxation, among other properties. By contrast, relaxation is much less common in the domains of work and nonwork obligation, but, then, we usually do not expect to find it there. Relaxation at work may take the form of *interstitial leisure*: short bursts of leisure activity like small talk with colleagues, browsing the Internet, or even reading a book. Such diversion can affect nonwork obligations as well. Author Joe Ryan once remarked that: "there's nothing to match curling up with a good book when there's a repair job to be done around the house." This observation suggests that a good book—for most people pleasurable reading—may be a more powerful source of procrastination than many other kinds of casual leisure such as taking a nap, watching television, or going out for a drive in the car.

Casual volunteering was omitted from the list of types of casual leisure set out at the beginning of this section. Still, some volunteers do read to children and people with vision-related handicaps, the service of the volunteers being no more skilled than the undemanding capacity to read aloud in the language of the novel or poem. Furthermore, reading here is not necessarily pleasurable, since the material may be too simple for the reader (e.g., parents reading stories to their young children, volunteers reading to kindergarten students) or simply not of interest to the reader (e.g. an eighteen-year-old volunteer reading to the elderly). Rather, the pleasure lies in the feeling of providing a needed and wanted service and the sense of involvement outside the family in the wider local community. All the same, these volunteers are reading, with much of the material they present being defined as pleasurable by their targets of this benefit.

PLEASURABLE READING AND INFORMATION/KNOWLEDGE

As a general rule, pleasurable reading is not conscientiously oriented to acquiring information or knowledge. The principle interest is usually intrinsic: to find enjoyment in the story being read. Nevertheless, there are four genres of reading that constitute exceptions to this observation: historical fiction, legend, biography/autobiography, and narrative nonfiction. The challenge for readers seeking both pleasure *and* information in these four is to try to separate fact from fiction. Other readers seem content to revel in the enjoyment that such material brings—in the story line, plot, quality of writing—and treat what they presume to be factual material as little more than interesting background to be accepted as written.

Historical fiction is, in this regard, especially beguiling. Historical fiction is a novel set in a specific period of actual history. In this genre information about actual events is not supposed to be fictive, not even incorrect. But how does the reader know that with certainty? Here the issue of trustworthiness takes center stage. Perhaps this is a problem to some extent for all of what we discussed as "edutainment." In consuming historical fiction its readers are entertained and educated in the same breath, just as they are when they view as edutainment such an exhibition in a science or history museum or watch a documentary. The latter normally come from an obvious authoritative source, however, whereas historical fiction is only as authoritative as its writer. This person may well be best known for the fictional side of this equation, as opposed to its factual-historical side. Consider as an example Philippa Gregory's *The Other Boleyn Girl* (2002), a historical novel centered on the life of Mary Boleyn, who was a sixteenth-century aristocrat in Tudor England. This book and its five sequels, which cover later time periods, have been alleged to contain some historical inaccuracies. Particularly those volumes set in the Tudor Age have been challenged, with critical reviewers being most upset with the fact that Gregory claimed complete accuracy.[6]

Legends are traditional stories, sometimes centered on a national or folk hero, which though based in fact, include considerable imaginary material. Since legends are collective creations, shaped and passed on over time by the people whose traditions they are, we would not ordinarily expect the same level of historical accuracy demanded of the single-authored historical novels. In other words, readers who consume legends as pleasurable activity typically gloss this veridical nicety; legends need only be believable, not verifiable. Still, readers of legends do acquire a sort of knowledge, even while commonly showing only limited interest in questions bearing on their accuracy and authenticity.

Biographies and autobiographies are true stories about real people written as books or as articles gathered together in a biographic compendium (e.g., the *Who's Who* series, The Encyclopedia of World Biography) . It is the book form that seems best suited to pleasurable reading. Written as a book or an article, the information conveyed is expected by readers to be as accurate as possible and the veracity of problematic data and observations duly noted. Here casual, pleasure-oriented readers seek enjoyment in information related imaginatively and engagingly in a narrative about a person's life. Whether this information is true does matter, much more so than that found in legend and historical fiction.

In other words, casual readers of biographies and autobiographies do not usually seek fulfillment in them, nor do they regard them as utilitarian literature. The facts are important, but only rarely do these readers seem interested in checking them out, challenging their accuracy, perhaps even impugning their relevance to the narrative, as would someone more analytically minded. Nevertheless, fulfillment could be, or become, a future aim of the present casual reader, as in teenage athletes who read the autobiography of a hero in their sport coming away with an unshakable determination to excel there. Initially, however, they probably read the book out of curiosity, expecting it to be enjoyable. Although its deeper messages were unexpected, they were presumably most welcome.

Narrative nonfiction is factual information presented in a format that tells a story. According to the website Writers and Editors this genre goes by many names, among them, creative nonfiction, literary journalism, and fact-based storytelling.

In short form, it's an alternative to the traditional newspaper pyramid structure (in which, if you lopped off the bottom part of the story, the reader would still have all the key information). With narrative nonfiction you don't present the main point in the first paragraph—compelling narrative keeps the reader reading to find out what happens, and the journey to the epiphany is half the point.[7]

Facts in this genre are supposed to be treated with respect, the story being built around them and employing the elaborations necessary to make it a pleasurable read. Often regarded as a kind of long-form journalism, narrative nonfiction includes memoirs (journals), accounts of disasters, some biographies, and a range of other popular interests. Some journalists are inclined toward such nonfiction, in part because it is free of the strictures of the daily deadline and the word limit, the bane of their usual occupational existence. A new source for short forms of such nonfiction is the Kindle Single, which features works of 5,000 to 30,000 words (the equivalent of 30 to 90 pages)—longer than a magazine article and shorter than a short book. How-to manuals, public domain works, reference books, travel guides, and children's books are not accepted for publication. Fiction and short novels, in depth how-to articles, self-help guides, biographies and profiles, essays and general ideas, human interest pieces, and personal memoirs are accepted. Obviously, the Kindle Single has much to offer casual readers, especially those who lack either the time or the desire to read a brick sized novel.

BENEFITS OF PLEASURABLE READING

Einstein's sweeping condemnation of pleasurable reading, with which we opened this chapter, overlooked the benefits of casual reading, even if one of its effects is "using the brain too little." Hedonism is hardly cerebral, but all the same it also contributes positively to our lives.

Chapter 2 contains a list of five benefits of casual leisure, enduring outcomes that can result from pursuing it. What do they look like when experienced through pleasurable reading? The first benefit considered was serendipity, which raises the question in the present chapter of whether pleasurable reading might result at times in chance discovery. I know of no research or other scholarly discussion devoted to exploring this possibility, but the following literary observers of reading as an activity allow, in effect, that it exists:

> "How many a man has dated a new era in his life from the reading of a book."
> —Henry David Thoreau, *Walden*

> "No tears in the writer, no tears in the reader. No surprise in the writer, no surprise in the reader."
> —Robert Frost

"I read for pleasure and that is the moment I learn the most."
—Margaret Atwood

"In books I have traveled, not only to other worlds, but into my own."
—Anna Quindlen, *How Reading Changed My Life*

"We don't want to feel less when we have finished a book; we want to feel that new possibilities of being have been opened to us. We don't want to close a book with a sense that life is totally unfair and that there is no light in the darkness; we want to feel that we have been given illumination."
—Madeleine L'Engle, *Walking on Water*

Given these observations, perhaps what should interest us is not only the presence of serendipity in pleasurable reading but also its absence. More particularly, when the reader experiences no serendipity, is that a sign of weak writing?

The second benefit on the list was edutainment, which having just been discussed, allows us to move to the third: regeneration or refreshment. To the extent that novels and short stories, both pleasurable and fulfilling, transport their readers to another world, it is plausible to argue that some regeneration takes place. This assumes, however, that such reading and its tendency to absorb have occurred in the interstices between periods of intense activity; that the reader is in fact in need of being recharged. Regeneration can also serve to remedy boredom, exemplified by the worker who returns home from a day's work at a tedious job eager to alleviate post hoc its stultifying effects by getting lost in a good book. The Browning quote earlier in this chapter shows another scenario for regenerating oneself, accomplished in this instance by reading to assuage *in situ* ongoing boredom.

The fourth potential benefit to come from participation in casual leisure follows from its role in developing and maintaining interpersonal relationships. Participating together in a casual activity can help the pair forge closer ties. Pleasurable literature can be an effective avenue for such bonding. Thus, people sometimes talk excitedly to friends and acquaintances about the books they are presently reading or have recently read, and such word of mouth can even launch the careers of previously little-known writers like the authors of *Fifty Shades of Grey* and *Wool*. A more enduring link between two people is established when one lends the other some enjoyable reading. This gesture, an endorsement of the excellence of the material by the first, helps strengthen the tie between them. Interestingly, even people who seldom discuss their reading with others may report being less lonely than nonreaders because of their sense of contact with others acquired by way of the printed word. Rane-Szostak and Herth's (1995) study of older adults supports this proposition.

Well-being is the fifth benefit that may accrue from engaging in casual leisure. Perhaps the greatest sense of well-being is achieved when a person develops an optimal leisure lifestyle. Pleasurable reading can contribute significantly to reaching this agreeable blend of work, leisure, and obligation by facilitating relaxation, regeneration, sociable conversation, and entertainment. In line with Hutchinson and Kleiber's (2005) findings, pleasurable reading as with other kinds of casual leisure can also help protect the self by buffering stress and sustaining coping efforts. The complete absorption in a good book is one mechanism by which such self-protection is effected.

CONCLUSION

Balancing the positive and the negative with respect to pleasurable reading is easier to talk about than to reach. A major facet of the problem is leisure's popular image in contemporary society, elements of which are anything but complimentary (Stebbins, 2012, pp. 98–99). Pleasurable reading is tarred with the same brush.

"For Satan finds some mischief still for idle hands to do," proclaimed Issac Watts some 300 years ago. Today negative views of leisure tend not to be this hostile toward hands not at work (though some observations on boredom come close; e.g., Brissett and Snow, 1993) but rather take a different tack. Thus, the work ethic of modern times stresses that a person should work hard and avoid leisure as much as possible (Stebbins, 2004a, pp. 24–29). Work is good, while leisure is not (although a little of it after a good day's work is acceptable). Indeed the history of leisure shows the different image problems leisure has had to face across the centuries.

Alternatively, leisure is sometimes seen today as frivolous, as simply having a good time, or, in the language of leisure studies, as casual leisure and the quest for hedonic experiences. The image of frivolity fades off into that of leisure as a waste of time, because frivolousness is believed by some people to lead to nothing substantial, notwithstanding the several benefits of casual leisure considered in this chapter. A related image is that leisure is unimportant, in the sense that there is little need to plan for it, that what we do in free time can be determined on the spot.

Finally, some leisure is deviant. Such activity, to the extent the larger society sees it in unfavorable terms while defining it as leisure, also contributes negatively to the latter's public image. Note, however, that the deviants themselves may not embrace this interpretation of their questionable activities. Note, too, that negativeness of the image is stronger in cases of intolerable deviance than in those held to be tolerable. Surely we would, for example, view with greater intolerance serial murder as leisure (Gunn and Cassie, 2006) than gamers' social construction of violent video game play as leisure (Delamere and Shaw, 2006). Even getting pleasure from reading about serial murder would probably raise eyebrows among certain people. And some women discreetly read erotic material, presumably in an attempt to avoid being labeled (tolerably) deviant because of their "prurient" interests.

The study of deviant leisure became more widespread in the 1990s (for a literature review see Stebbins, 2012, p. 99) What is important to observe with respect to the matter of leisure's public image is that deviant leisure may assume either the casual or the serious form (we have so far been unable to identify any project-based deviant leisure). Casual leisure is probably the more common and widespread of the two, though not always the more tolerable. The deviant serious pursuits, composed primarily of aberrant religion, politics, and science, are engaged in as appealing work or leisure. Thus many these pursuits are, in the main, taken up as liberal arts hobbies in which extensive utilitarian reading is required to learn their ideational foundation.

The checkered image of popular leisure lies in contrast to that of serious leisure, devotee work, and utilitarian reading. These are sketched in the colors of respectability, accomplishment, assiduousness, discernment, and the like.[8] Yet, in the popular mind, these pursuits, reading included, carry an image that is other than leisure. This imagery was considered earlier under the headings of utilitarian reading and reading textbooks in higher education. As a nonreading example, the neighbor of one of my respondents in the study of amateur archaeologists grimaced after hearing the first describe the fulfillment he gets from excavating a site: "Ouch! It sounds like work to me."

NOTES

1. Reading any of these genres with the aim of analyzing them, as many a scholar in literature and communication is wont to do is, as explained in the preceding chapter, to study this material motivated by utilitarian interests.

2. For the texts of over sixty famous speeches, see http://famousquotes.me.uk/ speeches.

3. This quote was found on drmardy.com (http://www.drmardy.com/metaphor/ welcome.shtml).

4. Book clubs are now informal meetings of people to discuss books, in contrast to commercial firms established to sell books, albeit often at a discount (such as Book-of-the-Month Club). Book-Clubs-Resource.com examines this distinction in its section on "What is a book club?"

5. See ReadThisToMe.org, which offers by telephone throughout North America a free reading service for the blind and low-vision community.

6. Source: http://en.wikipedia.org/wiki/The_Other_Boleyn_Girl. The eight historical inaccuracies listed here have been compiled from a variety of scholarly references.

7. Source: http://www.writersandeditors.com/narrative_nonfiction_57378. htm#bookmark1.

8. Note, however, that reading in deviant serious leisure does clash with the color of respectability. What would most people think of a person observed reading L. Ron Hubbard's *Scientology: The Fundamentals of Thought* or the Unification Church's *The Essentials of Unification Thought: Head-Wing Thought*?

FIVE

Self-Fulfilling Reading

The Liberal Arts Hobbies

The sagacious reader [is one] who is capable of reading between these lines what does not stand written in them, but is nevertheless implied. . . .
—Johann Wolfgang von Goethe, *Autobiography*

There are a multitude comments like Goethe's issued by authoritative observers bent on extolling the virtues of fulfilling reading. Some of them also apply to the fulfilling kinds of utilitarian reading, while all are meant to show directly or indirectly the writer's distance from, if not distaste for, what has been treated of in this book as pleasurable reading. And, sometimes, more broadly, such lines are intended to signal a rejection of casual leisure in its entirety. This is a stance commonly taken by intellectuals, reflected nicely in Radway's quotation in the preceding chapter. The opposing attitude is that such talk and writing are just another blast of academic snobbism.

One goal of chapter 4 was to show that, viewed through the prism of the serious leisure perspective, pleasurable reading does have numerous merits (some were portrayed as benefits). That chapter complements the present one, whose focus is on a distinctive type of reading-based serious leisure known as the liberal arts hobbies. In conceptualizing fulfilling reading as a singular kind of pastime, we can advance our understanding of it beyond snobbism, beyond the simplistic formula of reading as either high culture or popular culture.

THE LIBERAL ARTS HOBBIES

The liberal arts hobbies were introduced in chapter 2 as activities pursued by people eager to systematically acquire knowledge for its own sake.[1] If there is an LIS center in the domain of leisure, it is here; the area of free time where seeking information for intrinsic reasons is the supreme goal. As noted, many of these hobbyists search for information in a particular field of art, sport, cuisine, language, culture, history, science, philosophy, politics, or to a lesser extent, that of literature (referred to later more precisely as "belletristic fiction and poetry").[2] Furthermore, some of them are disposed to expand their knowledge still further through cultural tourism, documentary videos, television programs, and similar resources, activities that, since they are not reading, will be covered only sporadically.

The ever rarer Renaissance man of our day is also devoted to fulfilling reading. Such people avoid specializing in one field of learning to acquire, instead, a somewhat more superficial knowledge of a variety of fields. Being broadly well-read is a (liberal arts) hobby of its own. A retired colleague of the author who has set his sights on reading all the books written by Nobel Prize laureates is an example.[3] Another is provided by book collectors who, I am told by one of them, are most inclined to read what they have acquired. But, lacking research on this subtype, we will say little more about it in the present volume.

The liberal arts hobby is set off from other serious pursuits by two of its three basic characteristics: the search for a *broad knowledge* of an area of human life and the search for this knowledge for its *own sake*. Broad knowledge contrasts with technical knowledge, an admittedly fuzzy distinction based on degree rather than on crisp demarcation. Still, we can say that unlike technical, detailed knowledge, the broad kind is humanizing.[4] Through it we can gain a deep understanding and acceptance of a significant sector of human life (art, food, language, history, etc.) and the needs, values, desires, and sentiments found there. This understanding and acceptance do not necessarily lead, however, to amateur or hobbyist involvement in the sphere of life being studied.

Knowledge sought for its own sake implies that its practical application, if a concern at all, is secondary. Yet liberal arts hobbyists do use the broad knowledge they acquire. People enjoy expressing this knowledge, and the expression may be an important avenue by which they maintain and expand it. Elsewhere in serious leisure knowledge, which is often acquired through reading, is pivotal in finding fulfillment in the activity. Many times participants must have certain kinds of knowledge if they are going to produce anything of merit. Thus, aspiring stand-up comics avail themselves of various workshops, volunteer youth workers attend weekend training sessions, and old car collectors numerous manuals on maintenance and collecting. Likewise, amateur cooks are continually adding to the technical knowledge they need to prepare their meals well. By contrast, the liberal arts hobbyists who are fascinated by, let us say, the oriental cuisines will know a great deal about their ingredients, social significance, and methods of cooking, while being comparatively naive in the art of preparing and serving those same cuisines. To the extent that they are exclusively liberal arts hobbyists and not amateur cooks, they will lack the combination of artistry and technical knowledge needed to concoct and serve meals in the cuisines that have stirred their interest.

A third basic characteristic of the liberal arts hobby is the *profundity* of its broad knowledge; that is, such knowledge is more than merely entertaining. This characteristic, which is also found in the more technical bodies of knowledge associated with the other forms of serious leisure, is particularly relevant for the hobbyist whose passion is current politics. While searching for profound news analyses, this enthusiast must constantly strive to avoid or at least bracket the primarily entertaining and therefore rarely enlightening broadcasts and analyses of the political news heard on popular radio and television (Altheide and Snow, 1991, chap. 2). Mass media often provide entertaining but uninformative accounts of many such subject areas, and the hobbyist must search more widely to find satisfying information.

Acquiring Knowledge

Liberal arts hobbyists acquire their broad knowledge through *active* rather than passive learning, accomplished by intentionally seeking the desired ideas. In other words they share the orientation of other hobbyists who, instead of sitting back and waiting for their leisure experiences to come to them, take the initiative to define their own leisure needs and goals. Like other hobbyists, those pursuing a liberal art typically explain their attraction to it in self-interested terms, pointing for example to a desire to develop their personalities, intellectual capacities, or understanding of life. Many of these hobbyists can also be qualified as a notable category of lifelong learners. The main exception to the interest among the liberal arts hobbyists in acquiring knowledge are those whose passion is reading belletristic fiction and poetry, say, that of a certain author, country, or historical period. This area of liberal arts reading will be covered in the next section.

My research suggests that reading, chiefly in books, magazines, and newspapers, is the principal way in which hobbyists acquire their liberal arts knowledge. Observation shows that some amateurs are more inclined to read about their interests than to practice them. This pattern was notable in, for example, the distinction between amateur astronomers: some were strictly armchair astronomers who read about it but did no research; others were observational astronomers who actively collected data (Stebbins, 1980, p. 35). Others both read widely in their field and practiced it actively (Stebbins, 1993b, chap. 4), suggesting that amateurs and hobbyists may find time for a parallel hobby, namely, the one of acquiring a broad, liberal arts knowledge of their serious leisure pursuit.

As with pleasurable reading, book discussion clubs and commercial book services also play a role in fulfilling reading, though they are far less numerous than the groups that have sprung up around popular interests. Be that as it may, some public libraries run classic book clubs or similarly named groups, serious reading book clubs exist on college campuses and among friends, and there are many online forums for the discussion of fulfilling reading as well.

Reading can be substantially augmented by viewing or listening to news analyses and film and radio documentaries, listening to audio tapes and live talks, participating directly in activities related to the hobby, or engaging in a combination of these. The first two are self-explanatory. A main example of the third is found in educational travel. Of the fourteen tourist roles identified by Yiannakis and Gibson (1992, p. 291), only two—the "anthropologist" and the "archaeologist"—are compatible with our definitions of serious leisure and the liberal arts hobbyist. These anthropologists tour because they enjoy meeting local people, trying their food, and speaking their language. The archaeologists go on tours to view archaeological sites and ruins as part of their historical study of an ancient civilization. Many universities, professional groups, and travel companies offer educational travel courses and programs, and the Elderhostel program is a well-known example of this kind of travel. Tours can center on a city, culture, cuisine, and so forth. One type of subcategory are tours designed to impart knowledge in several of the liberal arts hobbies.

Whether travel for the purposes of direct participation qualifies as serious leisure depends in part on whether the pursuit of knowledge there is systematic and enduring. Lewis and Brissett (1981) observe that many contemporary vacationers who spend time in a different culture feel they must learn something about it, which does not imply, however, that they regard study of the culture as a hobby. A hobby is pursued over many years, not for just two or three weeks of holiday time. The same caution applies to the volunteer vacations described by McMillion et al. (2012), wherein the "vacationers" work without remuneration on projects in park management, trail building, archaeological excavation, reconstruction of historical sites, and a number of others. Such vacations can last up to two years, at which point some participants may want to terminate their interest in the project when it finally does come to an end. By this time it may have served as a stepping stone to remunerated work, realized a casual leisure interest in doing some sightseeing, or satisfied an altruistic desire to help humanity through volunteering. The one-shot volunteer vacation, at bottom, is usually a kind of project-based leisure, not a hobby.

Expressing Knowledge

Even though liberal arts knowledge is valued for its own sake, for its inherent fascination and enjoyment, hobbyists in this area may also want to externalize it in some way. Still, the motivation for doing this is complicated and remains to be studied systematically. For instance, such reading may discourage talking about it with others; it may be a self-contained experience not easily discussed or communicated. Perhaps the "exciting" material is morally suspect (e.g., an erotic novel, a macabre account), too much so to bring up in the reader's circle of friends.

For those who do want to talk about what they have learned, they do this because they find such knowledge prestigious, of interest to others, useful for making conversation, among other motives. At this stage in our understanding of the liberal arts hobbies, it is clear that two processes are at work in the expression of knowledge. One, by externalizing their knowledge of an art, science, or culture, hobbyists in these fields help themselves retain what they have learned. Two, in the course of external-izing the knowledge, they may discover new relationships and meanings in material they already know. Many a high school and university teach-er can attest the validity of both processes, having repeatedly seen them in operation during their involvements with students.

The processes of retaining knowledge and discovering new ideas are nowhere more apparent than when we express our capacity to use a foreign language. We learn the foreign language to read it or speak it, if not both. In the course of such reading and speaking, we further our facility in both areas, whereas if we did neither we would be unlikely to achieve even minimal linguistic mastery. It should be clear that this ex-pression is an essential step in the acquisition and maintenance of the language as a personal value, as a form of knowledge in its own right, rather than as a practical or instrumental application of it. For instance, a person might practically apply the language by seeking employment re-quiring its use. Alternatively, to serve an amateur or hobbyist interest, he or she might read scientific articles or listen to newscasts in it.

Talk appears to be the main way for liberal arts hobbyists to express their knowledge. And since the knowledge was acquired in leisure, it is most likely to be expressed there, notably in casual, sociable conversa-tions with friends and relatives, often sharing photos or audio recordings after a trip or lecture. Perhaps other ways exist too, these being depen-dent in some instances on the particular hobbyist or amateur talents these participants bring to their liberal art. Photography is one obvious applica-tion of this sort; others may include writing and painting. For some peo-ple one of these arts could be the main vehicle for expressing their liberal arts hobby, with talk being little more than an accessory.

THE LIBERAL ARTS HOBBYISTS

Having explored the general nature of the liberal arts hobbies, it is now time to consider each as a separate leisure activity. That is, what in particular do these enthusiasts do in the ten fields listed at the beginning of this chapter? Of course they read. But what special sources are available for them and what supplementary opportunities might they take advantage of? And by the way, it is possible that there are more liberal arts hobbies than these ten, a list that should be seen, in the spirit of social scientific exploration, as modifiable.

Art

This section covers the diverse fine and popular expressions of music, painting, sculpture, photography, theater, dance, in fact any aesthetic field capable of spawning a reading interest sufficiently deep and enduring to be considered a hobby. As discussed earlier, the popular expressions of these activities fall within the rubric of art, even though they are often labeled as mere entertainment. The art of writing will be taken up in the section devoted to belletristic fiction and poetry.

Hobbyist reading in the fine and popular arts comes in several forms. There are, of course, published books, often a substantial magazine literature, and now blogs and websites that offer substantive reading on the arts. Reading can focus on biographies of famous artists, nontechnical descriptions of how each art is produced, histories of these fields, individual works of arts, and sociological analyses of particular arts set in their sociocultural context. Books about geographical places related to art have become popular in recent decades and make good hobbyist reading (and visiting): La Scala (opera) in Italy, the Metropolitan Museum of Art in New York, Claude Monet's house at Giverny in France, and the Yasgur Farm in New York State where in 1969 the first Woodstock Music & Art Fair was held.

Sports

Hobbyist readers about this activity have arguably the largest selection of literature of all the liberal arts hobbies. Sports' immense worldwide popularity helps explain this wealth of leisure opportunity. Remember that sports is considered in the serious leisure perspective under three headings: amateur, professional, and hobbyist. Accordingly, though we lack survey data on the matter, it appears that most liberal arts hobbyists in this area are primarily interested in the professional wing. That is, they usually read biographies about professionals (which may include the pros' amateur years), historical accounts of professional sports teams, histories of a certain sport (including its amateur beginnings), chronicles of famous tournaments and playoff series, and possibly other interests. As in art there is also in liberal arts reading in this field a nontechnical interest in how a given sport is played. Sports-related books and magazines constitute the main reading sources, with pertinent articles turning up on occasion in other magazines and in some newspapers. Finally, it is probable that readers in all these sports either play them or are serious spectators of them, which may include some international travel to watch tournaments as well as famous players and teams.

The hobbyist sports, in significant measure because they lack a professional counterpart with its visibility and allure, offer much less reading for liberal arts enthusiasts. However there are still plenty of books, magazines, and websites and blogs for each sport, even less-widespread sports like orienteering and dogsledding.

Liberal arts hobbyists probably do not emerge in any significant number around every one of these amateur and hobbyist sports. Or, where they do exist, they are also likely to perform them. A main problem may well be the thinness of literature on some of the less-practiced sports like polo or horseshoes. It is possible, too, that some reading enthusiasts in sport concentrate on a category, such as all activities using some kind of racket or those carried out on foot over land, namely, long-distance running and race-walking.

Sports can be divided into four categories (Stebbins, 1998, chap. 3): team sport (professional), team sport (elite amateur), individual sport (professional), and individual sport (elite amateur). Defining amateurs and professionals in sport is an intellectual endeavor bristling with difficulties. Some amateur athletes devote themselves full-time to perfecting their athletic activity, much as real professional players do in every sport. Although professional both by definition and by level of competence, elite amateurs generally lack the visibility and respect enjoyed by true professionals. Still, these amateurs are highly influential in their own social worlds; here they are considered insiders by the much larger number of ordinary amateurs, the regulars.[5]

Cuisine

Every culture has its own cuisine, although these days with the globalization of practically everything, all but the most isolated of them has been modified by foreign influences entering as new ingredients, methods of cooking, and ways of preparing food. Liberal arts hobbyists in this area, however, seem not be interested in every cuisine under the sun, but only in the most celebrated. For these are the cuisines on which there is a voluminous literature, local opportunities exist to sample public and private exemplars, and a variety of aficionados with whom to talk shop. These cuisines are haute cuisines, in the sense that none in their cuisine bourgeoise form seems to have much hobbyist appeal. In approximate order of greatest interest as a liberal arts hobby, they are French, Italian, Greek, Moroccan/Lebanese, Japanese, Chinese, and Spanish. But, in fact, there is a good deal to read on the cuisine of any major country on the planet. Moreover, in many of these countries, food varies by region, giving thus scope for specialization or, alternatively, when taken together, a more complex understanding of the cuisine of an entire society. Nevertheless, books bearing on the cuisines of, for example, Ecuador, Libya, and Fiji are rare. Moreover regular, dedicated magazine coverage may be available in English only for French, Italian, and Greek cooking.

The greatest amount of reading in this liberal arts hobby is practical, written for another kind of hobbyist, namely, the gourmet cook (Hartel, 2006; 2010). Moreover, liberal arts hobbyists might be satisfied with this, for they do gain information on how to cook. But, instead of preparing a dish or a full meal, they analyze from this informational base a specimen of their cuisine served in a restaurant or private home. Thus the most informed may weigh in knowledgeably on the ingredients and cooking methods used, the sociocultural and perhaps historical significance of the dishes consumed, the presentation of the meal, and the level of quality of the entire undertaking. Yet others might well want more historical and cultural depth in which to frame such information. Some cookbooks include this, whereas others gloss it or mention it not at all. The latter, being utilitarian but with a practical slant toward accomplishing something, are not enough for readers searching for self-fulfillment in the acquisition of knowledge.

Language

Learning a foreign language is by its very nature a long-term activity. It is usually pursued through a combination of reading, oral tuition, and face-to-face conversation with other learners and competent speakers. Some of the information gained in these ways, especially at the beginning of the learner's career in this leisure, is highly practical, centered on vocabulary, grammar, spelling, pronunciation, and so forth. With competence in reading, the liberal arts hobbyist begins to explore various aspects of the culture in which it is embedded, for example, samples of its literature, art, cuisine, and popular activities.

Self-fulfillment gained from learning a second language comes via two main routes. One is mastery of the language itself: sufficiency in reading and speaking effectively in the target language. Hugo Durrant describes the powerful sense of accomplishment that comes with such mastery:

> So what is it about putting your French language learning into practice like this that is so exciting? A simple conversation like the one described above [held while renting a car in France], conducted in English as one's own native language, would be pleasant but hardly note-

worthy. What does make it so seemingly special, is the power that learning French gives you to enter an entirely new world that is separate from the one you normally inhabit.[6]

The second route is enculturation, or more precisely further enculturation, since to learn the language is to learn only part of a culture. Yet reading in the foreign language is a fruitful and deeply fulfilling way of becoming acquainted with its surrounding culture. Every culture can also be discovered in other ways, for example, by viewing it (e.g., dress, pictures, outdoor activities, architecture), hearing it (e.g., music, talk, urban traffic), tasting it (in its cuisine), and smelling it (e.g., not just the cuisine but the smells of manufacturing, pollution, even body odor).

Culture

All the liberal arts fields fall under the rubric of culture. That said, some hobbyist readers develop a passion for the culture of a particular country or region, like French Canada, Scandinavia, or the Middle East. Reading here is necessarily selective, in that the full culture of any country or region is too complex and extensive for one person to grasp. Still, some areas appear to be indispensable to a decent general understanding of any culture. These include art, dress, cuisine, history, religion, political system, built environment, and work and leisure, the exploration of which is aided by at minimum a tourist's knowledge of the written language.

The local language plays an interesting role in this hobby. For most countries and regions of the world, there is ordinarily in all these cultural areas a cornucopia of readings in English. Nonetheless, it is difficult to escape local terms, for often no translations exist for a country's holidays, geographic features, place names, key figures, food and eating habits, and so forth. Hence, liberal arts culture buffs find themselves spurred on by many of their own interests to learn something of the local language, for most a most pleasant requirement.

Again, book, magazine, blogs, and discussion groups on the target culture offer ways for hobbyists to explore their subject further.

History

History buffs constitute one of the largest groups of committed reading hobbyists. In addition to individual reading, hobbyists find resources through history clubs or societies or online groups. Groups may focus on many aspects of history: regions, art, sports, military history, technology, explorations, and the like. Local history is also a rapidly growing subject of amateur study.

Family history, as is evident, commonly gets grouped with local history. The first, however, is not a liberal arts hobby for the typical participant. Rather, this person's goal is to create a genealogy, a document outlining part or all of the history of the writer's family. To be sure, there is reading to be done here. But it is primarily utilitarian, as in searching official records for the dates of births, marriages, and deaths of ancestors and studying biographic sources to discover interesting (to the genealogist) aspects of their lives. In this case, it is most validly classified as a making and tinkering hobby, not a liberal arts hobby.

Science

Both the liberal arts hobbyists and their amateur counterparts seem mostly attracted to the visible sides of science, to phenomena they can actually or possibly observe without specialized equipment and training. In other words, they tend to avoid fields like chemistry and physics. Furthermore, the two sometimes join the same clubs, as was evident in my research on amateurs in archaeology and astronomy where enthusiastic scientists and readers mingled at the monthly meetings (Stebbins, 1980). We should expect to find this same composition of membership in equivalent organizations established for pursuing serious leisure in, for instance, zoology (especially birds and large mammals), meteorology, mineralogy, and botany (especially trees and flowers).

So hobbyist interests in science seem to revolve around phenomena that readers can easily observe locally (amateur astronomers observe locally distant celestial objects). Nevertheless, a few of them might become fascinated with elephants or lions while living in Chicago or grizzly bears and mountain elk while living in Cairo. Apart from what they can read at home and see at a nearby zoo, they might want to travel to Africa or the North American Rockies in an attempt to see these beasts in the wild. The African safari is one well-known way to help quench the thirst for this kind of knowledge.

As with the amateur scientists I have studied, liberal arts hobbyists appear unlikely to develop an interest in abstract scientific theory. Low-order explanations of interesting local phenomena are welcome and understandable, but reading in the more abstruse areas of the discipline is beyond the ken of all but a few. This is almost exclusively professional territory.

Bibliotherapy

Some people with difficult and lasting medical and psychological problems get introduced by their professional caregivers to a type of self-help literature designed to enhance their understanding of their condition and increase their capacity to live with it. Known as "bibliotherapy" it is possible to conceive of this activity as a kind of scientific reading hobby, albeit one with a greater than usual practical slant to it. That is, this is leisure—a sort of therapeutic recreation—to the extent that these clients or patients want to acquire and use such knowledge, while the knowledge acquired can be quite profound, extensive, and subject to change as the relevant sciences advance.[7]

Philosophy

While liberal arts hobbyists interested one or more sciences shy away from their theoretic end, those passionate about a philosophy or about the history of philosophy show a different propensity. Philosophy is necessarily abstract, though it should be noted that philosophers usually write about questions of interest to the inquiring mind (e.g., ethics, aesthetics, epistemology, and metaphysics). By contrast, pure mathematics—treated in this section as a branch of philosophy—is devoid of content of any sort; it is the ultimate mental playground for the abstract thinker and reader.

Hobbyist readers might center their attention on general philosophy, explored by reading an array of books on the subject some of which contain extracts from the writings of the greats in the field. Others might prefer to specialize in, for instance, moral philosophy or the philosophy of mind, language, or religion. Additional specialties include western philosophy, eastern philosophy, medieval philosophy, modern philosophy, and ancient philosophy. Then there are the philosophic traditions of existentialism, pragmatism, phenomenology, German idealism, and so on.

Books abound on these subjects; large public libraries are good sources and are likely to have more material for lay readers than university libraries. Online forums are also widespread for those who want to share comments about their readings with other hobbyists. BookTalk.org is a free book discussion group, book club, and online reading group with thousands of members and hundreds of forums. From time to time some of its participants read and discuss books on science and philosophy. Of interest, too, is BookTalk's list of banned books, which is composed of the 100 most frequently challenged books in a wide variety of fields published between 1990 and 2001. Finally, there is no shortage of online and live discussion groups the meetings of which commonly revolve around a philosophic reading chosen in advance (search Google using "philosophy discussion groups").

Politics

The reading buffs in politics, who may be partisan, are nonetheless in constant search of the most reputable up-to-date reports and analyses of political events. Readers try to determine which books and periodicals are respected for their reportorial accuracy and analytic acumen. The ordinary, popular news media are often avoided because their reporting is too often inaccurate and their analyses too often questionable or unconvincing.

Politically oriented reading hobbyists may be biased toward a conservative or liberal viewpoint, but they still seek impartial, factually-sound-as-possible information about the political scene, so as to optimally inform the stand they take on particular issues. In other words, the liberal arts hobby of politics is not purely an intrinsic pursuit, but rather one pregnant with practical implications for its enthusiasts. These hobbyists, by reading deeply in this area, also strive to be contributing citizens at the geographic level of their interest. At bottom, when they vote, write letters to the editor, speak with political candidates and incumbents, and so forth, they are contributing to the democratic process in their society,

And speaking of the geographic level of the political reading hobby, it can vary from local to state/provincial/regional and on to national and international. Some hobbyists have the time and interest to become properly informed at all levels, while others restrict themselves to the local or state/provincial levels or, often it appears, to a combination of the two. Depending on the level the sources of impartial, scientifically sound information vary considerably. For local politics, hobbyists mainly rely on magazines, newspapers, and Internet sources that carry reliable reporting. On the national and international planes, the political reading hobbyist is drawn away from the popular press toward its intellectual, "serious news," "quality press" complement, exemplified in English at its highest level by, among a few others, The Times (London, UK), The New York Times, The Economist, and The Guardian.[8] For both local and national/international politics, discussion groups also play a role.

Belletristic Fiction and Poetry

Belles lettres is the realm of fine-art, high-culture fiction and verse as well as its criticism and analysis. For sake of efficiency I will label as *belletrists* those for whom reading in this area is a hobby.[9] Of all the kinds of reading covered in this book, belletristic fiction and poetry is where consumers are the least inclined to speed read. It makes no more sense to rush through these works than to bolt down, as if on the run, a finely prepared meal of French cuisine or tour in quick time all the displays in New York's Guggenheim Museum.

Belletrists read slowly and carefully for several reasons. One of them is that they want to relish the artistry of the writing. The reader dissects the text of the novel or poem, reveling in the words, sentences, and figures of speech of the author, but pondering as well how these creations might be different. In belletristic fiction the reader mulls over the plot and subplots contemplating their intricacy, trying to anticipate how they will unfold, marveling at the imaginative way each has been constructed, and the like. Belletrists also give considerable thought to the characters in the work, to the author's description of them, their relationship with each other, their fit with the plot, and so forth.

Belletristic fiction and poetry often convey one or more messages. Consider Charles Dickens's *Bleak House* which contains a stinging critique of the dysfunctional, outdated English Chancery court system operating during the middle nineteenth century. William Faulkner's *Light in August*, published in 1932, communicates a harsh condemnation of, among other prejudices of the day in the American South, those against women and black people. German Nobel Laureate in Literature Günter Grass, whose poem "What Must Be Said . . ." (written in German) about nuclear Israel and Iran is a modern instance of politically charged artistic writing (Kulish and Bronner, 2012). Such examples show the high level of profundity that these literary messages can attain, while providing yet another dimension along which belletrists may appreciate a particular work.

Given the artistry of belletristic writing and the communication of profound messages by this means, it is no wonder that discussion groups meet, commonly on a monthly basis, to talk about selected exemplars. These can meet in person (privately with friends or acquaintances or at a library or college) or online.

The practice of rereading parts of fulfilling passages was examined in chapter 3, the intent there being to underscore the frequent need to study utilitarian material. Such may also be done with belletristic fiction and poetry, as when a reader wants to review an intricate aspect of the plot or reflect on the implications of a metaphor that has just been encountered. Furthermore, with such material, there is also an inclination to admire again the passages that stand out for their literary artistry. Belletrists, having learned what fine writing looks like, want to bask in its every moment.

It follows that, of all the different types of liberal arts hobbyists, the readers of belletristic novels and poetry are the least likely to find information in their material. Nor do they usually expect this to happen. Granted, they need information about where to find that material, how to join discussion groups, who to rely on for informed analyses, and the like. Yet such searching takes place outside the core activity of reading a fine novel or poem; the first has extrinsic value whereas the second is valued for its intrinsic (emotional, aesthetic, imaginative, clever, etc.) properties. The second is about having a deeply enriching experience, whereas the first is about acquiring useful knowledge, even if it does sometimes engender an emotional reaction (e.g., pleasure, excitement, respect, disappointment).[10] In their essence, the first is a rational set of means-ends links, whereas the second is an affective mosaic of feelings, sentiments, imaginings, and reactions to these three. This is what Goethe had in mind in his epigraph at the head of this chapter.

LIFESTYLE

From what has been said so far about the liberal arts hobbies, it follows that the ways in which knowledge and understanding are acquired and expressed in them result in a distinctive set of lifestyles for the hobbyists. These lifestyles have no real equivalent in the other forms of leisure, whether serious or casual. This is because the liberal arts hobbies are for the most part individualistic undertakings. And in harmony with this preference, social worlds in these hobbies tend to be comparatively minimal. Learning a language is the principal exception.

People learning a new language inspired by the hope of advancing to a level where they can easily read and speak in it *must* enter in a profound way the social circles of those who are fluent in that language. My research on the Franco-Calgarians for whom French was their second language demonstrated that, as learners, their port of entry into this social world was ordinarily achieved by way of, in the first instance, certain language courses and the institutions offering them. During this phase of learning the language they had only superficial contact with the social milieu of the city's francophones. Later, based on their increased linguistic fluency, some of these students deepened their involvement in the local francophone social world by frequenting its clubs, bookstores, cinemas, restaurants, travel agencies, and festivals and special events. In turn these contacts produced a small but growing number of French-language friendships, acquaintanceships, and network ties. It also provided some with an opportunity to work as volunteers for one or more francophone services or events. Other students who had the time and financial means achieved the same end by entering a local francophone scene elsewhere in, say, Quebec or France.

Yet language as a liberal arts hobby associated with a well-developed social world is an anomaly. Other liberal arts hobbies appear to be only weakly organized in social worlds. They are nevertheless sometimes social; the foregoing section in which we examined the expression of the liberal arts hobbies shows the validity of this assertion. But the manner of acquiring these hobbies is generally individualistic, centered primarily in reading and secondarily in some sort of viewing and listening. The closest most of these hobbyists typically come to entering a social world is when, to advance their interests, they take a noncredit course, participate in an educational travel program, or join a discussion group. But usually they enroll only sporadically in the first two, if for no other reason than acquiring knowledge in this manner is seldom inexpensive. Moreover, unlike the clubs, restaurants, and bookstores patronized by the foreign-language hobbyists, the courses are evanescent. For this reason alone they make comparatively poor rallying points for those pursuing serious leisure of this type. The discussion group, this chapter demonstrates, is in this respect the exception.

In short, the lifestyle of many liberal arts hobbyists is, in its acquisition phase, reclusive. Close friends and relatives might even portray them as to some extent antisocial. Still it is probable that these hobbyists would describe themselves and their leisure in more flattering terms such as being peaceful or relaxed. Moreover, we can say that theirs is an exceptionally flexible type of serious leisure. It can be carried out at the convenience of the person, molded around other activities, obligatory or not, and accommodated to the demands of work and family.[11] Scheduled courses, lectures, and radio and television programs sometimes momentarily compromise this flexibility, but with reading as the main method of acquisition, rigidizing leisure lifestyle for this reason is relatively rare.

Serious reading does require a "study" of some kind. The knowledge being acquired is complex and profound; it often takes considerable time to understand it fully and integrate it well with what the reader already knows. The tendency toward reclusiveness in these hobbies is partly explained by the need "to get away from it all" to think about the many facts and ideas. People without a study would probably find the liberal arts hobbies difficult to pursue effectively and satisfyingly. Be that as it may we shall see in the next chapter that all sorts of places can be turned into studies, the quiet room at home possibly being only the most common. Many hobbyists can read well in a tranquil place in a city park, on a front porch, or at a public library. In the sense intended here it is the absence of inescapable and incapacitating distraction that is the essence of a study.

The liberal arts hobbies can be elitist, and in an earlier era were often thought to be exclusively so (e.g., Pieper, 1963, p. 36; Veblen, 1953, p. 252). Still, present-day observations suggest that these hobbies should not be universally described this way. It is true that participation in some of them requires exceptional financial resources (e.g., to travel widely, purchase books, take noncredit courses). Given such requirements people with modest incomes may be excluded. Yet, to the extent these same people can participate by using the public libraries, searching online, listening to radio and TV, and subscribing to one or two periodicals in their field of interest, the liberal arts hobbies are in reality accessible to a wide range of social classes. And of course some zealous enthusiasts are inclined to spend every extra penny they possess on their leisure passion. Even the inherent "intellectual" quality of the liberal arts hobbies may turn out, upon closer examination, to be much less restrictive than we would predict. In fact, past research has, with a few exceptions, discovered a lack of association between social class and many other forms of serious leisure (Stebbins, 2007a, pp. 61–62).

CONCLUSION

The liberal arts hobbies are far from the style of leisure currently being touted by the promoters and enthusiasts of exercise and physical activity. Although people actively participate in liberal arts hobbies in the sense of using their own initiative, what they do is largely sedentary (though some may have separate hobbies that are more physical). For some, their liberal arts hobby may, so far as the realm of leisure is concerned, be their only possible fulfilling central life interest. The liberal arts hobbies should be especially attractive to those with physical limitations, although adequate sight and in some activities taste or hearing are important preconditions for truly satisfying participation.

In brief, when considered together, the liberal arts hobbies do appeal to a wide segment of the community. Additionally, they offer a special place in the world of serious leisure for people who are bodily unable or psychologically unwilling to pursue more physically demanding activities. Based on this broad appeal and the previously mentioned ease of financial access to many of these hobbies, they may be accurately described as one of the most egalitarian types of serious leisure.

Since people who pursue a liberal arts hobby usually interact too infrequently to generate a richly evolved social world, it is reasonable to conclude that their collective contribution to the wider community will be different from that of the amateurs, career volunteers, and other hobbyists. The latter three, as I have pointed out elsewhere (Stebbins, 1992, pp. 118–20), contribute to the integration of society in part through the highly evolved social worlds that spring up around their serious leisure. Although the liberal arts hobbyists are in a weaker position to contribute to societal integration in this important way, they are, however, in a much better position to contribute in another way, a way that is equally important. More precisely, they contribute through their deep humanistic understanding of the culture and behavior of another category of humankind. As stated earlier in this chapter, humanistic knowledge, unlike technical, or detailed knowledge, begets a deep understanding and acceptance, although not necessarily adoption, of a major sector of human life (art, food, history, language, etc.), of the needs, values, desires, sentiments, and the like that are found there.

Ovid wrote in *Ex Ponto II* that we should "note . . . that a faithful study of the liberal arts humanizes character and permits it not to be cruel." Should a need for one exist, this is a key moral justification for pursuing the liberal arts hobbies in modern times, when world stability is threatened by our intolerance and misunderstanding of those who differ from us. Finally, Ovid's words justify research on this neglected subtype of serious leisure. Indeed they would even seem to exhort us to get on with the job.

NOTES

1. For a discussion of the methodological foundation of this approach to the liberal arts hobbies, see Stebbins (1994).

2. The intellectually oriented followers of politics, although they may be committed to certain political parties or doctrines, nonetheless spend significant amounts of time (and possibly money) informing themselves in this area of life. To be a hobbyist here, one must pursue knowledge and understanding; one must do more than merely claim, however fervently, to be of such and such a political stripe.

3. The books are mostly written by the laureates in Literature, which is nonetheless a hefty undertaking given that the first prizes were awarded in 1901.

4. Hence the designation of liberal arts, as used in the sense of the arts branch of university education.

5. Insiders and regulars in the social worlds of the serious pursuits were introduced in chapter 2.

6. http://EzineArticles.com/481133.

7. Bibliotherapy is a term fraught with multiple meanings, only one of which, though reasonably prevalent, has been employed here. Additionally, there is some hint in the vast literature on the subject that reading, in general, can be therapeutic, a point briefly addressed in chapter 6.

8. The demarcation of tabloid and broadsheet is especially evident in local journalism, but only rarely works out to be the equivalent of popular and intellectual found at the national/international level. In other words, many local broadsheets compete as they must with the tabloids also strive to be popular, while failing substantially to meet journalism's intellectual, serious news standards.

9. This definition is narrow, expressly created for the ends of this book. For belletristic writers, as a category, may pen not only belletrist fiction, poetry, and criticism but also literary essays. The latter are omitted from this section, because they form an organic part of many readers' lists in other liberal arts hobbies such as politics, history, and the arts.

10. Ross (1999) explored this affective dimension of readers' involvement with their material, arguing that such contact is part of the research agenda of LIS (see chap. 2 in the present volume).

11. On the question of the flexibility of hobbyist leisure and the social isolation of participants in certain types of it, see Olmsted (1993, pp. 30–31).

SIX

Reading in Everyday Life

The pleasure of all reading is doubled when one lives with another who shares the same books.
—Katherine Mansfield

Reading like prayer, remains one of our few private acts.
—William Jovanovich

These two quotations capture well a central characteristic of liberal arts hobbyist reading: its inherent reclusiveness mixed with a consuming desire to talk to, or hear from, others about its interesting, often, exciting content. This reclusiveness-gregariousness paradox becomes a leitmotiv in the present chapter, recurring time and again as we cover the circumstances of reading, the reading lifestyle, and the social world of reading. Committed reading of all three motivational types arouses these two contradictory tendencies, which are, however, most obviously and extensively at work in the domain of leisure.

CIRCUMSTANCES OF READING

Under the title of, for want of a better term, the "circumstances of reading," I will deal with its ease, convenience, affordability, and enduring effects. Also covered in this section are two threats to reading, one new, one old: scamming e-books and censoring books of any kind. Finally, here is where we examine the environments in which reading typically occurs.

Ease

The concept of ease of reading centers on its how quickly and smooth-
ly serious leisure participants can enter into this activity. The concept's
importance is evident in the comparisons it enables across the spectrum
of free-time activities. First, note the ease of most reading, seen in simply
picking up a book, magazine, or newspaper and immediately perusing
its content. Some people may also have to put on reading glasses, switch
on a light, or, for e-reading, turn on an electronic device. Ease, as conceived of in this discussion, does not refer to acquiring reading material,
which in fact is not always easy.

Ease is part of what attracts people to certain serious pursuits. In
juxtaposition lesser ease compromises attractiveness, while sometimes
also being downright demanding. Examples include donning and sometimes preparing sports equipment (e.g., ice hockey, American-Canadian
football, cross-country skiing), warming up for physical activity (e.g.,
music, ballet, wrestling, weight-lifting), and generating mental readiness
(e.g., getting "psyched up" to perform optimally a theatrical role, musical
concerto, or sport position). The greater ease of reading has its parallels
in, for instance, knitting, wood working, creative writing, and stamp collecting.

The level of ease of involvement with a serious pursuit falls thus along
a continuum. Reading and some other passions are attractive, in part,
because of their greater ease of entry into the core activity. Activities
entered with lesser ease are probably not disliked intensely for this reason, but if nothing else, they foster a nagging worry that these prelimi-
naries if not done well could adversely affect the core activity once
underway.

Convenience

Convenience refers to the level of portability of reading material.
Books, magazines, and newspapers are intentionally designed to be
handy, with pocket books and tabloids being handier than hard covers
and broadsheets. Books that are relatively unhandy—heavy, thick, large
format—may be scorned for their clumsiness. It is no accident that e-
readers are convenient. Online databases have somewhat replaced the
need for microfiche and microfilm searches for serious scholars, access to
which was difficult and involved no portability.

The main component of convenience is portability, and portability has
been transformed by e-readers. Although subject to breakage in a way
that hard-copy books aren't, readers can read them at a mountain lake,
take them up a mountain trail, or hold them easily on a packed commuter
train.

Storage is another component of convenience. When not being read books, newspapers, and magazines must be kept somewhere. Does the reading material fit decently on the bedside table, breakfast table, reader's desk, coffee table in the living room, or other furniture? Material read on a computer may pose a problem, in that the bigger laptops may be too large for the space in these areas or the occasion of their use. What happens to the breakfast conversation when one of the interlocutors is substantially eclipsed by a computer screen?

Affordability

Some hobbyist readers dish out sizeable sums to feed their voracious appetite for material. The reason for the popularity of the bargain paperback is obvious here, as it is for affordable electronic and Internet material. Nevertheless, some readers love the hardcover editions, their feel, their comparative elegance, their durability, and the like. The price of these "treasures" may be barely affordable, but for them sentiment overrides economics.

The circumstance of (un)affordability drives some readers to the library, to borrow from a friend, to copy material (perhaps illegally), even to shoplift it. Others buy electronic copies, though they might prefer a "proper" book or magazine. Still others turn to the used-book market, buying online or, more interestingly, hunting in the half-light of the musty brick-and-mortar, second-hand outlets. Bookstores may even become part of the "must-sees" during a reader's touristic travels; for example, while holidaying in London why not explore some of its many second-hand book shops or, in Paris, some of its *bouquinists* lined up along the Seine?[1]

Enduring Effects

To establish habits based on reading circumstances is to establish a main part of the pleasurable and liberal arts reader's lifestyle. Dictated by what we can or will pay for reading material joined with the levels of ease and convenience we have grown accustomed to, committed reading soon begins to assume a certain pattern. On this matter we lack data, but it seems reasonable to speculate that some of these hobbyists read most consistently at bedtime, whereas others do so at lunch, on the train, Saturday or Sunday afternoon, and the like. What is read and when may also become routinized, as in reading the newspaper at breakfast or a pleasurable novel in bed before falling asleep.

Does utilitarian reading lend itself to such patterning? Probably not. This motivational type is mostly reading on demand, determined by the requirements of work or nonwork obligation. It must be done sooner or later, and doing this in installments, which is how people usually read a novel in bed or at lunch, is often neither necessary nor possible. As noted earlier utilitarian reading can be fulfilling, even if our choices about when it is done are usually limited. The range of flexibility in this type is evident in the scholar's approach to reading monographs and journal articles vis-à-vis that person's approach to reading a technical report written as background for a committee meeting soon to take place. The first can be postponed to some extent, whereas the second has a clear deadline.

Threats

Scamming has come to the happy realm of committed reading, arriving by way of the Internet and then only very recently. Book purchases can be carriers of viruses, and fake websites can take consumers' credit card information for criminal purpuses. The usual threats of censorship also plague readers today.

The censoring and banning of certain books is as old as the scamming of any book is new. In recent times the Nazis censored a variety of American books dramatized by publicly incinerating them. Salman Rushdie's *The Satanic Verses*, published in 1988, was censored in early 1989 by Islamic fundamentalists in Iran who also burned it in public as well as issued a *fatwā* calling for his execution. Kelly (2012) discusses censorship and book banning in American schools. In the past, books were banned because they were considered anti-white, used profanity, portrayed rape, and described pigs mating and being slaughtered. She goes on to examine the different strategies for banning books in schools, after which she presents teachers with recommendations on how to avoid becoming embroiled in a censorship battle.

So reading certain material is sometimes felt to be bad for the mind and at times, by implication, bad for society. Apart from "warping" a person's mentality, the material may also be defined as grounds for unwanted activism. And activist tendencies do exist in some of the liberal arts hobbies, being most likely to surface from reading in art, science, politics, and language.

The fact that some books might be targeted for censorship because they advocate activism is tied up with another aspect of committed reading. Serious readers focused on music or history might militate for better training opportunities or more public financial support in these areas. Reading hobbyists in science might join the chorus of those pushing for improvements in science education or in recruitment of students to this branch of learning. Such advocacy, at times controversial, illustrates yet another facet of the gregarious side of reading.

Reading Environments

The concept of reading environment refers to the physical and sensory situations in which committed readers read. That is, these situations include not only the physical setting but also, to the extent the reader perceives them, music, nearby conversation, sounds of nature, adequacy of lighting, even certain smells and tactile sensations. We turn first to the physical settings.

In the main in Western society reading takes place in the following settings: home, work, parks, waiting areas, public transit, long-distance trips, bars and restaurants, libraries, and possibly others. The setting or settings chosen depends on a multitude of factors bearing on the material being read and what the reader hopes to gain from it.

Reading at home is arguably the most frequent setting for this activity, if for no other reason than most people spend more time there than anywhere else. Furthermore, we are most likely to have significant control over this environment, in that we may be able to insist on a readable level of ambient noise, find a reasonably tranquil space, negotiate lighting to our advantage, set temperatures suitable for sedentary activity, easily and relatively cheaply find food and drink, and so forth. Additionally, a fireplace with a crackling blaze or a back garden with chirping birds can enhance the domestic reading experience with some delightful sounds and smells. Nell (1988, p. 250) found that reading in bed is common: "It is private time and, like play, it stands outside ordinary life. For many readers, it is the only time of day they can truly call their own."

Home reading may be motivated by any of the three types. This is less true at work, however, where in occupations requiring committed reading, the utilitarian variety dominates. There in private offices workers, some of them occupational devotees, digest reports, research documents, technical books, and the like. There occupants have, they hope, sufficient control over the conditions that sustain concentration (e.g., noise, lighting, temperature), starting with being allowed to shut the office door. But countering this tactic some organizations try to enforce an open-door policy, leaving workers important enough to have their own office to face interruptions. In short, utilitarian reading can be fulfilling, but at work the conditions nurturing this reward may be far from ideal.

Critical in utilitarian reading is following the argument of the material. Here readers are carried through it by the logic of that argument rather than by the unfolding of plot, one of the essential elements of both the pleasurable and the belletristic novel. In other words, with utilitarian material readers must keep track of the reasoning with which it is structured, a process that demands close concentration and, it follows, a close-to-ideal reading environment. In popular the plot is clear enough to carry the reader along without recourse to complex logical relationships. In more complex novels, a highly intricate plot constructed from a complex web of characters, events, ideas, and things requires concentration equal to that required by a complex scholarly argument.

Parks can be wonderful places to read, graced as many are with trees, flowers, singing birds, and possibly a fountain or small pond. But they can also abound with distractions, running from raucous visitors to noisy maintenance operations. Wind and rain can add to a reader's woes as this person seeks favorable conditions for committed reading. Given these circumstances it is probable that most reading attempted in parks is pleasurable rather than serious.

Reading, talk, and sleep are the three main activities in waiting areas, which include such the spaces adjacent to professional and commercial offices; those in airports, bus stations, and ferry terminals; and those serving public transit. Few people come here to read, but to alleviate the boredom forced on them by obligatory waiting, some wind up doing just that. Reading conditions are rarely even decent in these places, for there is often distracting talk, annoying loudspeakers, disagreeable antics of some of the others who are also waiting, and a general movement of people. In the waiting areas outside professional and commercial offices, magazines may be provided, but the same barriers to concentration pertain should the would-be reader be fortunate enough to find an article worthy of sustained attention.

Reading in waiting areas is one challenge, whereas reading on public transit can be quite another. Committed readers become engrossed in their book or magazine article, which might result in missing their stop. Those who try to read while standing on a commuter train like great bunches of asparagus have their work cut out for them. With one hand firmly grasping a support and the other clutching some reading material, they must somehow turn its pages pushed into their chest by the crush of bodies. No wonder the Kindle is popular.

Reading on airplanes is ordinarily a dramatically different experience, especially the long flights during which passengers have enough time to devour an entire (usually pleasurable) book of moderate length. True, distractions are possible here, too (e.g., official announcements, crying babies, loud and loquacious neighbors), though on, say, a trans-Atlantic flight they usually disturb only a small segment of it. Moreover, seasoned travelers with serious reading interests probably equip themselves with sound-deadening head sets.

The practice of reading in restaurants includes bars and coffeehouses used for this purpose. Although these places are rarely established with this function in mind, their owners and managers seem not to intentionally discourage it.[2] Instead, the second two, especially, have been conceived in the desire to promote interaction among customers. Reading, the individualistic activity that it is, runs counter this social goal. Here the aforementioned reclusiveness-gregariousness paradox finds concrete expression. And when coffeehouse proprietors hold poetry readings, these events may be understood as attempts to resolve it.

The public library is in some ways the quintessential reading environment, though a case might be made that it is, rather, the reader's home. But, unlike home, the traditional raison d'être of the library is the provision and perusal of reading material (and now aural and other visual material as well). Everything is, or at least is supposed to be, organized around these two goals. This includes lighting, noise levels, reading facilities (chairs, desks), necessary conveniences (toilets, water fountains), and the like. Still, some patrons may be annoyed by the rules prohibiting food and drink, by the possibility of theft of personal belongings, or by the off-putting habits and oddities of others nearby, including such obtrusions as coughing, sniffing, exuding body order, and muttering to oneself. Obviously, the optimal environment for committed reading is delicate; the requirement of concentration enforces many conditions that nonserious readers and people who read little or not at all fail to recognize or, if recognized, fail to respect.

Other Environments

Many of the other environments have already been covered in the preceding section as they bear on the spaces they could possibly affect. Yet to be discussed, however, are the effects of ambient music. This new musical category is intended to provide a kind of white noise for readers by filtering out the background noise that inhibits it. The music is supposed to be unobtrusive, in depreciatory tones it is supposed to be wallpaper music. On the website Yahoo7Answers, responses were mixed to the question of "Do you listen to music while reading a book?"[3] Some of the respondents do listen, others do not, some identify their preferred reading music, and others say they concentrate unintentionally on the music rather than the book. One of the conditions favoring concentration, for those who find some music to be good for their reading, is that the music be dreamy. The rhythmic stuff draws attention, while some so-called dreamy music would probably command the attention of a trained musician or liberal arts music hobbyist. Another condition is the profundity of the text (e.g., complicated information, rich plot, imaginative writing). Since committed readers often go in for such material, background music of any kind may well weaken their concentration on the first.

Consideration of these other environments also raises the issue of multitasking while reading. Can readers engage simultaneously and effectively in both their reading and the use of certain other media? An investigation of students in middle school and high school conducted by the National Endowment for the Arts (2007, p. 8) found that 58 percent of the sample enjoyed other media while reading. More precisely, the students reported using these media during 35 percent of their weekly reading time. During 20 percent of their reading time they also watched television, played video or computer games, did some instant messaging, read and sent e-mail letters, or surfed the Web. This study failed to distinguish among the three motivational types of reading considered in this book, leaving us to wonder how its findings might have varied accordingly.

READING AND LIFESTYLE

Near the end of the preceding chapter we examined the lifestyle of the liberal arts hobbyist. The aim of this section and the next one is to expand that discussion to the lifestyle of committed readers in general, as readers, workers, and people occasionally faced with certain nonwork obligations. The goal is to identify some of the key strategies that these readers follow in their search for overall lifestyle favoring this serious pursuit. The strategies are finding solitude, committing time, and working to develop an optimal leisure lifestyle.

Solitude

The need for and the actual finding of solitude were considered in the preceding section, albeit in rather desultory fashion. So by way of generalization I now wish to observe that committed reading is commonly done in solitude or, if done in the company of others, this state is achieved by tuning them out. Tamora Pierce illustrates this tactic well in the following passage from her novel *Briar's Book* (chap. 2):

Tris: I was reading.

Sandry: You're always reading. The only way people can ever talk to you is to interrupt.

Tris: Then maybe they shouldn't talk to me.

Solitude, actual or virtual, is a condition for serious reading, which however, rests on the process of finding that condition. As is evident in the preceding section, readers try to tune out not only other people but all other distractions. Moreover, Tris is in effect pointing out that committed readers have rules they expect people who know those readers well to abide by, one being to conduct no conversation with them while they "have their nose in a book." Another is, when within range of a reader's hearing and seeing, to minimize intrusive activity. It is in finding solitude that we strive to shape our lifestyle such that reading can be pursued with maximal reward.

Time

Another key strategy directing the pursuit of committed reading is to set aside of time to do it. Here we can see personal agency in action, manifested in the *discretionary time commitments* that readers make. The latter concept refers to the noncoerced allocation of a certain number of minutes, hours, days, or other measure of time that a person devotes, or would like to devote, to carrying out an activity (Stebbins, 2006). Such commitment is both process and product. That is, people either set (process) their own time commitments (products) or willingly accept such commitments (i.e., agreeable obligations) required of them by others. It follows that disagreeable obligations, which are invariably forced on people by others or by circumstances, fail to constitute discretionary time commitments, since the latter, as process, rest on personal agency, on one's proactivity. In short, discretionary time commitment finds expression primarily in leisure and devotee work.

Note, however, that we can, and sometimes do, allocate time to carrying out disagreeable activities, whether at work or outside it. Such commitments—call them *coerced time commitments*—are, obviously, not discretionary. Hence, they fall beyond the scope of this discussion and, with some interesting exceptions, beyond the scope of the serious pursuits (i.e., some of the costs in serious leisure and devotee work can be understood as coerced time commitments—see chap. 2).

Generally speaking the serious pursuits require their participants to allocate more time than participants in others forms of work and leisure, if for no other reason vis-à-vis those other forms, than that they seem most likely to be engaged in over the longest span of time. In addition, certain qualities of the serious pursuits, including especially perseverance, commitment, effort, and career, tend to make amateurs, hobbyists, volunteers, and occupational devotees especially cognizant of how they allocate their free time, the amount of that time they use for their serious pursuits, and the ways they accomplish this.

The discretionary allocation of time in leisure is, then, hugely complicated. So when broaching the subject we must be sure to specify the form and, within the form, the type of leisure or work in question. Time allocation differs substantially from amateur boxing to hobbyist barbershop singing to volunteer fire fighting and from genealogical projects to casual people-watching from a street-side cafe. Complexity of allocation of leisure time may also be affected by significant others. Not infrequently such allocation must be negotiated with spouses, partners, friends, and relatives. The leisure participant may want to devote more time to an activity than these people will countenance, given that the latter want the former to spend time (and perhaps money) with them. Enter the issue of uncontrollability discussed in chapter 2, which engenders in those who are passionate about a serious pursuit the desire to engage in it beyond their available time or money.

In this regard reading has its own, often idiosyncratic, patterns of time allocation. Because of its exceptional ease and convenience, reading enthusiasts can, as noted above in the section on enduring effects, establish their own patterns of reading as they participate in the three domains of life. One of the great appeals of leisure, compared with most work and nonwork obligations, is the relative freedom it gives us to do what we want to do when and where we want to do it. Sure a variety of constraints make this freedom less than complete (for a review see Jackson, 2005), sometimes seriously so. Yet leisure and devotee work are essentially uncoerced kinds of behavior fashioned by the individual participant within a limiting set of constraints. In this bittersweet context, reading juxtaposed with other uncoerced activities nevertheless offers readers extraordinary freedom to pursue their passion.

Moreover, for them, this constitutes all or part of a foundation on which to build a highly attractive lifestyle. This possibility is especially pertinent for certain social categories, among them people who are elderly, have physical handicaps, or are temporarily ill or incapacitated. Often severely limited in what they can do physically, reading (and being read to) emerges as an appealing remaining choice. For example, Luyt and Ho (2011), in a review of the literature on reading among the elderly, cite evidence supporting the observations that for them this activity promotes relaxation and social interaction, helps satisfy curiosity, and generate a sense of social responsibility often effected by spreading to others around them important information acquired by reading. Harrison and Gravelle (2008) found in their small sample of palliative care patients with cancer that reading facilitated escape from their daily hardships. The activity also took on new meaning from what it had before they contracted the disease.

Leisure Lifestyle

In constructing a leisure lifestyle, people try to blend and coordinate their participation and allocation of free time in one or more of the three forms. They attempt to organize their free time in such a way that they approach, as they define it, an "optimal leisure lifestyle" (OLL). The term refers to the deeply rewarding and interesting pursuit during free time of one or more substantial, absorbing forms of serious leisure, complemented by judicious amounts of casual leisure or project-based leisure or both (Stebbins, 2000). People find optimal leisure lifestyles by partaking of leisure activities that individually and in combination help them to realize their human potential, leading thereby to self-fulfillment and enhanced well-being and quality of life.

People searching for an OLL strive to get the best return they can from their free time. What is considered best is, of course, a matter of personal definition; a quality of the OLL predicated on the individual's awareness of the great range of possibly available activities. Thus people know they have an OLL when, from their own reasonably wide knowledge of feasible serious and casual leisure activities and associated costs and rewards, they may say they have enhanced their well-being by finding the best combination of the two forms.

People enjoying an optimal leisure lifestyle are aware of other appealing casual and serious activities but sufficiently satisfied with their present constellation of activities to resist abandoning them or adopting others. Still, this could change in the future, as an activity loses its appeal, the person loses the core ability to do it, or new activities gain in attractiveness. From what I have observed in my own research, people with OLLs seem to sense that at any point in time, if they do try to do too much, they would force a hectic routine on themselves, risk diluting the rewards of their leisure, and thus become unable to participate as extensively in what has been profoundly worthwhile.

Voluntary Simplicity

The voluntary simplicity lifestyle has gained adherents in recent decades. In a book entitled *Voluntary Simplicity* Duane Elgin (1981), who was heavily influenced by Gandhi, writes that, among other things, it is

> a way of living that accepts the responsibility for developing our human potentials, as well as for contributing to the well-being of the world of which we are an inseparable part; a paring back of the superficial aspects of our lives so as to allow more time and energy to develop the heartfelt aspects of our lives.

The voluntary simplicity movement, which also goes by the denominations of, among others, "simple living" and "creative simplicity," was launched in the mid-1930s with an article written by Richard Gregg (for bibliographic information on the several reprinted versions of this article, see Elgin, 1981, pp. 297–98). The idea may be much older, however, as suggested by the following: "Better is an handful with quietness, than both the hands full with travail and vexation of spirit" (Ecclesiastes 4:6).

Given that, in pursuing either serious leisure or project-based leisure, participants make many contributions to the community (the "world" in the Elgin quotation) and that these two forms offer two avenues for realizing human potential, it is reasonable to interpret participation in such leisure as consistent with the principles of voluntary simplicity. Furthermore, the two do share the common ground of encouraging and fostering self-fulfillment through realizing individual human potential while also contributing to the well-being of the wider community. For the typical, true votary of voluntary simplicity, this may mean paring back work activity, where such activity brings in more money than needed for the simple life and uses up time that could be spent in self-fulfilling leisure.

What makes voluntary simplicity and committed reading natural partners is, in part, because the second may be carried out with little significant financial outlay. Unless a reader craves expensive hardcover books, magazine subscriptions, and worldwide tours of sites that support this person's reading interests, such activity is—as leisure activities go— quite inexpensive. For those so inclined they can pursue it as one kind of more or less "non-consumptive leisure" (Stebbins, 2009b, pp. 118–26). This confirms their allegiance to the voluntary simplicity movement while belying the unsupportable claim that leisure is purely a matter of consumption, little more than purchase of a good or service (e.g., Cook, 2006, p. 313).

THE SOCIAL WORLD OF READING

It was stated in chapter 2 that the ethos of the serious pursuits—it is one of their six distinguishing qualities—is composed substantially of the social world that grows up around those activities. In this present section we explore in greater detail the social worlds of committed readers, doing so according to the four types set out by Unruh (1979; 1980): strangers, tourists, regulars, and insiders.

In the world of reading, *strangers* are those who participate little in the leisure activity itself but who nonetheless contribute enormously to making it possible. These are essentially those involved in the business side of reading: publishers, printers, distributors, libraries, websites, book fairs, software developers, and the like. One need only ponder the convenience of downloading an article or entire book to understand the crucial role that this part of the social world plays for the typical modern reader. The earliest of all these players is, of course, the bookstore, which existed as far back as ancient Greece. Today, it is mostly at these establishments that book launchings and signings are held, constituting special occasions where readers and authors may meet however briefly. Book festivals, held all over the world on a regular basis, offer this as well.

Tourists are temporary participants in a social world; they have come on the scene momentarily for entertainment, diversion, or profit. Most amateur and hobbyist activities have publics of some kind, which are, at bottom, constituted of tourists. Still readers, as suggested by the reclusiveness-gregariousness paradox, may well exhibit among the serious pursuits the weakest manifestation of this type. Readers are among the audience at an author's public reading. But they are not really tourists as just defined. At bottom, we must ask if it is possible for something as private as reading to attract temporary participants interested in playing the role of tourist.

Nevertheless, readers can certainly be *regulars*, or the people who routinely participate in the readers' social world. This is the gregarious side of their lifestyle, wherein they attend author readings, participate in book discussion groups (formal and informal), chat with friends and relatives about interesting books and articles, and so on. Being a regular in the social world of reading means participating on the business side of reading, and today this usually involves online ordering or browsing. It can be much more personal, however, when done in a small independent bookshop, where personnel are often eager to discuss their goods with customers. These smaller establishments along with libraries may also become rallying points for some regulars, hangouts where they recognize each other as committed participants in this serious pursuit and with whom they sometimes discuss mutual interests. It is also common for public libraries to run book discussion groups and courses on reading, some of them specialized by genre (Styles, 2007, p. 45).

Still, being a regular also has to do with the reclusiveness of reading, of engaging routinely in the activity as framed in the pattern of time allocation that, over the years, the individual has arranged for it. There may even be a social element here, as readers negotiate with other people to find sufficient time, space, and peace to pursue effectively this kind of leisure or devotee work. Otherwise, regulars who are able to read for lengthy period of time must, to rest the mind from its concentration, take the occasional break. This pause may become routinized, as in heading to the kitchen for coffee or a snack, accomplishing a short alternative activity (even one that is disagreeable), going for a brief walk, perhaps even conversing for a few minutes with someone.

The *insiders* engage in the same core reading activities as the regulars, while standing out from them by showing exceptional devotion to the social world that both types share, to maintaining it and to advancing it. Reading insiders include those who, among other achievements, have outstanding reading and analytic skills, have a remarkable record of materials read, and read assiduously and voraciously. They may also be the most inclined toward activism, to rally with others in support of the interests of their literary passion.

Communication

Social worlds are not formal organizations, but they are nonetheless organized. In the world of reading this is accomplished primarily by certain means of communication such as websites, emails, newspaper announcements, and so on. We look here at three prominent means of social organization for readers: tribes, information dissemination, and book clubs. They all attest the gregarious side of this pursuit.

A communicative arrangement in the social world of reading that involves some regulars is finding membership in a *tribe* related to their literary interest. This metaphor, elaborated by Maffesoli (1996), identifies and describes a postmodern phenomenon that spans national borders. It is thus much broader and more sociological than its anthropological precursor. Maffesoli observes that mass culture has disintegrated, leaving in its wake a diversity of tribes. These tribes are fragmented groupings left over from the preceding era of mass consumption, groupings recognized today by their unique tastes, lifestyles, and form of social organization. Such groupings exist for the pleasure of their members to share the warmth of being together, socializing with each other, sometimes seeing and touching each other, and so on, a highly emotional process. In this, they are both participants and observers, as exemplified by in-group hairstyles, bodily modifications, and items of apparel. This produces a sort of solidarity among members not unlike that found in certain religions and many primitive tribes.

Today, more than fifteen years after Maffesoli published his monograph, many modern tribes are held together by the Internet, with only very small groups of members ever meeting face to face. Any immensely popular book on an international scale—for example, J. R. R. Tolkien's *The Lord of the Rings*, Stieg Larsson's, *The Girl with the Dragon Tattoo*, Dan Brown's *The Da Vinci Code*—tends to develop a tribe-like following of readers who keep in touch with some of their kindred spirits by way of blogs, text messages, and, locally, face-to-face exchanges. Some of these literary tribes are sustained, in part, by fan websites such as the Lord of the Rings Fanatics Network or Kate's Book Blog on *The Girl with the Dragon Tattoo*. Fans can gather in subsections of larger, general-reading websites as well, as in the chat rooms and clubs that exists on GoodReads.com. Fans can discuss their opinions of novels, from likes and dislikes to serious analysis to issues of historical accuracy.

The process of disseminating information about books and magazines is of utmost importance in the pleasurable and self-fulfilling types of this leisure pursuit. Most inveterate readers in these two types are constantly searching for new material, which they do through various Internet services, publishers' circulars and catalogues, posters and flyers available in bookstores and libraries, book jackets, and other means. A number of contemporary authors maintain their own websites, where readers may go for information on forthcoming works, sales promotions of in-print volumes, and possibly even commentary by critics and ordinary readers.[4] Additionally, many of today's readers use their social media to convey opinions about books they and their friends have read, sentiments that sometimes contrast sharply with the hype given to those volumes by their publishers (*The Economist*, 2012b).

A discussion of the social world of pleasurable readers would be incomplete without mention of the Book-of-the-Month Club (BOMC), on which Janice Radway (1997) has provided some unique data. Today, the BOMC, now a subsidiary of Time Warner, offers its members a monthly selection of popular fiction or top nonfiction, which they may decline, at substantial discounts from the publishers' retail prices. Radway labelled as "middle-brow" the books commonly purveyed by this organization. A principal goal of BOMC she learned is to ferret out exciting pleasurable reading, reading that is not "academic" or "high culture," reading that will therefore attract and retain large numbers of subscribers to the service.

CONCLUSION

Committed reading lacks glamour. Unlike some sport, art, entertainment, and hobbyist activities, the act of reading—this pursuit's core activity—is nearly always done without fanfare. Of all the serious pursuits it must be as close as any to being a purely intrinsic activity. In other words, the reclusiveness pole dominates, though more so in pleasurable and self-fulfilling reading than in some of the utilitarian reading.[5] For participants who want to "strut their stuff," exhibit their leisure accomplishments before a (hopefully) admiring audience of some kind, they must seek a pursuit capable of attracting that kind of attention. Being on a football team, in a civic orchestra, among the artists at a community exhibition of Sunday painters, or among those volunteering at the municipal zoo, for instance, mixes the intrinsic appeal of executing these activities with the extrinsic appeal of social recognition that such execution can bring.

Not so with most committed reading. Moreover, the private nature of this pursuit has become the fount of some negative images about it, expressed as "book worm," "nose in a book," even "bookish" when used to describe pedantry or book learning as inferior to real experience. This is not to argue that, among the general population, committed readers are seen as a special class of deviant. Yet, if their only substantial passion in life is reading, they might be thought of as eccentric. They may even see themselves in these terms (Nell, 1988, pp. 6–7). There is a hint of such imputations in the exchange between Tris and Sandry presented earlier.

Such observations raise the larger question of the place and worth of committed reading in contemporary Western society. We have spent a lot of time to this point examining its value for the individual, which I believe we must conclude is considerable. And perhaps that is justification enough, for after all one of the main rewards of utilitarian and self-fulfilling reading is extensive personal development. And relaxation achieved by way of pleasurable reading is hardly an insignificant adaptation to the frenetic pace of today's world.

NOTES

1. The real enthusiast might want to travel to Hay-on-Wye near the Welsh border renowned for its approximately thirty secondhand and antiquarian bookshops nestled together in one of the town's neighborhoods.

2. Owners of coffeehouses have had their problems with readers and users of computers, some of whom buy a cup of coffee and then monopolize a table for a couple of hours or more. This practice slows the turnover of customers, in turn reducing the margin of profit needed to succeed in a small business with slim profit margins (see Alini, 2009).

3. Source: http://au.answers.yahoo.com/question/index?qid=20070124155326AAMTIu, retrieved 6 April 2012.

4. Advertising is much more infrequent and low-key for utilitarian reading, as seen in publishers' catalogues and websites, mailed circulars, and publicity insertions in periodicals. Furthermore, such utilitarian reading as reports and newsletters contain very little publicity at all.

5. For example, academics must occasionally discuss with colleagues and students the research literature they read. They must also speak about this literature when presenting papers at conferences, giving talks at academic and research establishments, and answering questions from reporters or other interviewers bearing on the diverse practical implications of their expertise.

SEVEN

Conclusion

Reading and Society

Reading maketh a full man, conference a ready man, and writing an
exact man.
—Sir Francis Bacon

A number of themes have emerged over the preceding six chapters,
themes that beg further consideration within the conceptual framework
of this book. That framework is constituted of the four types of committed reading and three types of motives for such reading all as pursued
and expressed across the three domains of life. We engage in this kind of
reading for the experience and knowledge it can bring us. Moreover, its
effective pursuit depends mightily on a wide range of practical information about reading material and related events. Our theoretic foundation
for exploring these types and their interrelationship in the everyday
world of readers has been library and information science (LIS) and the
serious leisure perspective (SLP).

The emergent themes to which I want to address myself in this chapter are (1) reading and its relationship to writing; (2) abandonment of
reading; (3) reading as an excuse for inaction; (4) reading as a substitute
for the real world; (5) reading, obesity, and physical activity; (6) reading
as a catalyst for life reorientation; and (7) reading's contributions to the
community. In covering these themes, discussion will be confined primarily to the sociological and social psychological levels of analysis as
observed in Western society. The main object of this chapter is to place
reading and the emergent themes in the three domains of work, leisure,
and nonwork obligation.

READING AND WRITING

Writing is not a necessary extension of reading. Reading hobbyists know what good writing looks like and deeply appreciate it, but often do not ordinarily aspire to it as another serious pursuit. One caveat for the committed reader is that to try to become an amateur writer is to allocate a substantial amount of time to that goal. In this re-arrangement of daily lifestyle, the amount of time available for reading could well be seriously compromised.

On the other hand, writers of pleasurable and belletristic material, as with artists of every stripe, must get to know the accepted and renowned expressions of their art. That is, all artists must immerse themselves in the exemplars of their aesthetic calling and thereby gain a keen sense of how its canons are applied. The artists then use this conceptual and aesthetic background as a springboard for their own creative efforts and their drive to establish one or more unique expressions of the art. William Faulkner put it this way for writers:

> Read, read, read. Read everything—trash, classics, good and bad, and see how they do it. Just like a carpenter who works as an apprentice and studies the master. Read! You'll absorb it. Then write. If it is good, you'll find out. If it's not, throw it out the window.[1]

This is not to say, however, that writers, or for that matter other kinds of artists, also turn into hobbyist readers. Rather the first usually read only what is necessary to form and guide a career in their art and, to the extent that they heed Faulkner's advice, their preparatory program is rather unspecialized. For instance, do writers of modern American belletristic novels read the works of all their contemporaries? This seems improbable. But you can bet that a liberal arts hobbyist specializing in this area has already done, or intends to do, exactly that.

Be that as it may, committed readers motivated by utilitarian interests and writers of the material they read have a somewhat different relationship. It is unusual for readers of pamphlets, manuals, and textbooks to aspire to write these types of literature.[2] But it is different with the readers of scholarly and professional monographs and journal articles. Here lies the closest link between committed reading and writing as serious pursuits, for many readers in these endeavors are forced to write propelled by their intense desire to succeed in them. In the academic world this ukase finds expression in the sour apothegm of "publish or perish." Returning to Francis Bacon's epigraph it appears he was right to see readers and writers as separate literary creatures with contrastive goals.[3]

WILL READING BE ABANDONED?

This question, if posed around 1980, would have been received with derision and branded as utter nonsense. How could we ever get along without the four types of committed reading material, not to mention what we have called cursory reading and detailed ephemeral reading? To start, it seems highly improbable that cursory and detailed ephemeral reading will cease, nor will the committed reading of manuals and pamphlets. All four meet the practical need of acquiring certain kinds of information, for which there is no substitute. Thus, if you want to assemble the IKEA sofa-bed you just bought, you do so at your peril should you plunge ahead without reading the accompanying instructions.

But what of the other kinds of committed reading? Here, too, when practical concerns are foremost, as they are in utilitarian reading, there is no replacing it. There is no substitute for reading a journal article or committee report. And people who refuse to read them have not found a substitute, but rather are prepared to carry on without the information contained within. This leaves us then with the possibility—some would say the spectre—of abandoning pleasurable and self-fulfilling reading. In this scenario people who have learned to read would still read when necessary in the aforementioned practical areas of work and nonwork obligation, but would eschew leisure reading, serious and casual.

The putative causes of this decline are the electronic distractions inventoried in chapter 1. This possibility goaded Kernan (1992) to write on the "death of literature," doing so at a time when these distractions were fewer and used more infrequently than today. Nevertheless, Kernan could still blame our "electronic culture" for this decline, while also examining many other forces at play in this transformation. Now these distractions—the presence of ever more sophisticated electronic devices for sending and receiving messages and for being entertained—pose an ever greater threat to concentration on reading that requires this frame of mind.

Such an argument, if followed to its logical conclusion, suggests that technologically distracted readers would abandon pleasure and self-fulfilling reading fueled by an incapacity to satisfyingly engage in it. This, in response to the blitz of distractions undermining the reader's attempt to follow adequately a plot, story line, passage of subtle reasoning, and so on. This, in response to the desire for a level and rate of hedonic entertainment, which committed readers oriented thus would be denied to some degree.

The argument is plausible. But does empirical evidence exist to support it? We saw in chapter 1 that adults are reading these days, although the data and conclusions are flawed by inadequate conceptualization (e.g., crude measurements of what constitutes reading, usually that centered exclusively on the pleasurable variety). Moreover, it was pointed out in the preceding chapter that, more generally, adults are quite capable of leading an optimal leisure lifestyle consisting of a personally enriching balance of casual and serious activities of, for example, entertaining e-talk *and* something fulfilling like sport, science, collecting, making something, or—committed reading. Remember that the typical American adult has around 63.2 hours a week for family, leisure, and nonwork obligations.

It may even be too early in the history of the mass use of electronic devices for fun and need to draw solid conclusions on the effects of reading. Some text-messaging, for example, is deadly serious as when parents remain in touch with children away from home and vulnerable to the usual array of urban dangers. Shannon (2007) has pointed out that text messaging was born in late 1992 in England but the surge in its popularity is far more recent. In short, we cannot say yet with empirical conviction that (committed) reading risks being abandoned.

READING AS AN EXCUSE FOR INACTION

The charge that a person's desire to do more reading is but a subtle excuse for inaction is probably most justly directed at those who read for utilitarian reasons, in that they are attempting acquire information they believe will be useful. The question is whether they act on what they have learned or continue to search for more information, presumably to delay the day on which they will have to apply the information in some way. This, it appears, is only a problem where utilitarian readers find substantial self-fulfillment in what they peruse, and for this reason, find it difficult to set it aside to act on what they have learned. Additionally, the action that these readers are supposed to engage in, compared with the preliminary reading, lacks appeal.

To return to academia again, does the above scenario not describe the scholar who loves conducting the literature review, the stage in a research project that typically precedes the collection of data and their subsequent analysis? Indeed, these people adore so much this kind of reading that they not only digest all there is to read that bears directly on the study being mounted but also take numerous interesting side trips into other bodies of literature only tangentially related to it. These scholars are at heart a kind of liberal arts hobbyist ("reading maketh a full man") rather than an amateur or professional scientist or humanist (whose writing "maketh an exact man").

Nevertheless, it was observed earlier that some liberal arts hobbyists—especially those in art, science, politics, and language—*do* swing into action as activists in their area of interest. Examples included militating for improvements in science education and increases in funding for the fine arts. As a tentative generalization I suggest, then, that most readers are act two types, preferring to gather knowledge or experience literary excellence, with only a minority of them moving on to act three where they attempt to resolve a problem based on the utilitarian information they have read.

READING AS A SUBSTITUTE FOR THE REAL WORLD

George Bernard Shaw once complained that "what we call education and culture is for the most part nothing but the substitution of reading for experience, of literature for life, of the obsolete fictitious for the contemporary real." In line with the preceding section, the inveterate reader who fails to act misses out on the related experiences that action might have brought. Other committed readers miss out on experiences not related to what they are reading, because they have chosen to read rather than venture into the "contemporary real." Thus, the adult who reads the whole evening does not walk with friends, play amateur baseball, practice the piano, make a sweater, or tinker with an old car, among hundreds of other possible leisure activities.

Be that as it may, reading motivated by any one or two of the three types does produce its own set of *vicarious* experiences. So, from a preliminary run through the instructions, you can imagine what it will be like to assemble the IKEA sofa-bed. Then, as you actually assemble it, you have the complementary experience of finding pieces, turning screws, pounding in pegs, following the sequence of assembly, and so forth, which some people like (it is leisure) but others loathe (a non-work obligation). By contrast, readers of a novel can vicariously experience the goals, machinations, emotions, set-backs, discoveries, and the like of its different characters. But à la Shaw they cannot actually have those experiences (though, in their real lives, they might have lived through some parallels to them).

Shaw and a number of other observers maintain that it is bad to replace with reading the real experiences of life. That is, they conceive of the world of fiction as artificial and, for that reason, of little utility when it comes to getting around in daily life. First, note that this criticism can apply only to reading for pleasure or self-fulfillment. Utilitarian reading by definition pushes its consumers toward some kind of action (i.e., experience). Second, experience may be replaced in the present by reading, but that reading may subsequently become the wellspring of valuable experiences in the future.

READING, FITNESS, AND OBESITY

Reading is a sedentary activity (we might say "inactivity") and is therefore one of the targets of the active-living movement and its companion the lose-weight movement. Both operate under the banner of health promotion. Watching television and playing computer games are the principal *bêtes noires* of these two movements, with reading advanced as an additional reminder that any sitting or lying around when done in excess will have adverse effects on the human body.

Notwithstanding these views, the causal link between sedentariness and obesity lacks convincing scientific data, the literature on the subject being defined as at "an early stage of development" (Poortinga et al., 2011). Nevertheless, Judson (2010), an evolutionary biologist, argues that there is an established link between sitting, the position in which most people read most of the time, and weight gain. It is better to move in some way while reading, with even fidgeting being an improvement over absolute motionlessness. This might be a difficult prescription for committed readers, however, for their high level of concentration could very well lead them to forget to move or even fidget.

So the villain in the low fitness and high obesity drama is not reading per se but sitting or otherwise moving too little while occupied thus. And it is also obvious that some committed readers are both fit and svelte, a condition traceable to an advantageous combination of genetic heritage, healthy diet, and active work or leisure pursued beyond the hours spent with a book.

Again, utilitarian reading is probably less conducive to harmful sedentariness than its pleasurable and fulfilling counterparts. For instance, manuals, once read, often demand physical action of some sort and possibly some active, a priori inspection of the material with which the reader will have to work. When compared with books, journal articles are short, reasonably quickly read, and therefore easily put aside for something requiring mobility, like going to class, the library, or one's postal box to check the mail. Even reports are not usually so riveting as to lure their readers into a protracted period of insalubrious inactivity. By contrast, a good novel, pleasurable or fulfilling, has a magnetism that can attract for hours, pulling the reader into the plot and its characters with its imaginative style and language.

AS CATALYST FOR LIFE CHANGE

It is worth requoting Thoreau's observation here, namely, "that many a man has dated a new era in his life from the reading of a book." More generally, all pleasurable and fulfilling reading and some utilitarian reading, in principal, hold the possibility of redirecting a reader's life. In the utilitarian sphere manuals and pamphlets would not ordinarily be thought of as having so momentous an impact, whereas textbooks and especially scholarly literature could certainly be this potent. The crucial point is that committed readers open themselves to influences flowing from the text, some of which may bring a new dawn.

Without considerable exploratory research on the subject, it is difficult to typify these catalysts. Nonetheless, some examples can help adumbrate this area of inquiry. For instance, people committed to reading scholarly material might discover in a journal article or research monograph a new direction for their intellectual career. And how many students have discovered their occupational destiny upon reading a section in a textbook that discusses this fresh possibility?

Turning to novels, author Rowan Williams, when asked by *The Guardian* to reveal his literary inspirations, wrote:

> I read Patrick White's *Riders in the Chariot* when I was about 19, and it has been decisive in shaping my sense of what faith and ethics are and aren't. It was the first novel I'd read that dealt directly with the Holocaust. It was a novel about mysticism that challenged me profoundly about what I meant by God.[4]

Writer A. C. Grayling, in responding to the same question, said: "I'll reluctantly limit myself to three: Immanuel Kant's *Critique Of Pure Reason* in philosophical respects, Robert Tressell's *The Ragged Trousered Philanthropists* in political respects, and Tolstoy's *Anna Karenina* for what literature can mean and do."

READING'S CONTRIBUTIONS TO COMMUNITY

Committed reading, as with many other serious pursuits, can leave its mark on the social and cultural life of the community, be it felt locally, regionally, nationally, or internationally. Community is a vast subject, however, and by no means all possible aspects of it have been brought to bear on the serious leisure perspective in the name of that framework. There has nevertheless been research or discussion, sometimes both, on family, work, gender, and the wider community, each of which shows how committed reading can have social ramifications. We turn first to family.

Family

In the following paragraphs "family" is used as a summative term for spouses, partners, boyfriends, girlfriends, and other members of immediate or locally available extended family. At times, to be sure, such global treatment of the subject will not do, at which point discussion will become more refined.

My research on amateurs routinely covered the relations the respondents had with their families as these bore on their serious leisure (see Stebbins, 1992, pp. 108–11). The aforementioned concept of uncontrollability was born of these discussions, signaling that family relations may, on occasion, become contentious and testy over such issues as expenditure of time and money on the leisure activity in question. From such conflict talk of divorce sometimes arose, which was sometimes followed by dissolution, the serious leisure of the respondent being cited as its primary cause.

But the same research on amateurs suggested that serious leisure may also have a favorable effect on family life. For example, it can contribute to stronger bonds between two or more people when all share an interest in an activity ("a family that plays together stays together"). The serious leisure of one member may become a rallying point for other members, as in the parent or spouse who supports (in this instance as an agreeable obligation) the amateur, hobbyist, or volunteer involvements of the participant. Furthermore, the sense of well-being generated by much of serious leisure can favorably affect the family, in that the participant is as a result content, high-spirited, and possibly more accepting of others in the household.

The relationship of reading and family life can be complicated. For example, Ablow (2007) examined the Victorian claim that novel reading can achieve the psychic, ethical, and affective benefits also commonly associated with sympathy in married life. She looked into the ways in which novels in the mid-nineteenth century were believed to educate or reform readers and their marriages. Two centuries earlier John Bunyan wrote *The Pilgrim's Progress* (first published in 1678) the inspiration for which sprang partly from his new wife. She "came of godly parents, and brought two pious books of her father's to her new home, the reading of which awakened the slumbering sense of religion in Bunyan's heart, and produced an external change of habits."[5]

There is no equivalent research on casual or project-based leisure in the family, that is, research done under the heading of these two forms. It is likely that much of what has been observed for serious leisure could also be observed for these two, albeit differently manifested. Thus, a husband can, in the eyes of his wife, spend too much time before the television set, at the neighborhood pub, or reading pleasurable fiction, provoking in this manner frequent marital spats. By contrast, both could enjoy time spent together at the cinema, going out for dinner, or reading the same novel punctuated by conversation about it. In general, compared with its serious counterpart, casual leisure is less regimented, less bound by rules and schedules; it provides fewer opportunities for family conflict in this sphere of life. But the relationship of family and casual leisure is vastly understudied, so little can be said here that is not speculation.

It is likewise with project-based leisure, for no research exists yet on its relationship to family. There is reason to expect differences, however, for its limited duration could help keep conflict to a minimum. Family members might well reason that it is better to avoid contesting a member's involvement in a project that is due to end soon, especially if that person gains some fulfillment from it. Moreover, the possibility exists that other members might participate in the same project, giving all concerned a shared, appealing, leisure interest. Or the project might benefit one or more members of the family, as would knitting a sweater for someone, building a stone wall in the backyard, or developing the basement of one's home. Reading projects appear to be uncommon, they being most likely to consist of utilitarian reading of the kind needed as background for preparing a genealogy, gathering information on a tourist destination, making something from a kit (one with detailed instructions), and the like. In all three instances family members might be well served by what the participant read.

Work

My research on amateurs also routinely covered the relations the respondents had with their jobs as these relations bore on their serious leisure (see Stebbins, 1992, pp. 111–14). Conflict here has been found to be infrequent, though serious leisure participants of all types try to avoid work that could create major tension with their free-time passion. In the hobbyist field this was especially evident in a study of the three mountain activities of snowboarding, kayaking, and mountain climbing, where many of the respondents not only sought work having flexible hours but also pointed out how much more exciting and interesting their hobby was compared with that work (Stebbins, 2005b, pp. 108–11). Still, we may say for serious leisure, in general, that one's livelihood comes first in any showdown between the two.

But what about leisure enjoyed at work, as opposed to work undertaken during free time? Reading at work for pleasure or fulfillment presents an exceptionally convenient leisure opportunity while on the job. Chapter 4 contained a short discussion of free-time activity at work pursued as *interstitial leisure*, defined as uncoerced activity that occurs sporadically in short spaces of time stolen from what is formally recognized as work time, but informally converted by employees into leisure. Pleasurable and fulfilling reading are popular ways of using these minutes, though many other activities are also possible, among them, crocheting, texting, surfing the web, and simply daydreaming.

Looking at participation in serious leisure from the managerial standpoint, McQuarrie (1999; 2000), in a unique set of studies in this area, examined the issue of organizational support for employee commitments arising from their serious leisure (e.g., time off to present a noon-hour play, travel to a distant city to run a marathon). Her results showed that the amount and type of organizational support for such employee commitments vary widely. Moreover, she found that positive organizational support for serious leisure had a positive influence on the job-related attitudes of employees. She discovered, further, that supervisors and co-workers differ in their level of support for such leisure, with the latter being more encouraging than the former. All this is very well and good, but seems not to apply to committed, pleasurable and self-fulfilling reading, however much the latter type can develop the person. Given the image of committed reading considered at the end of the preceding chapter, such activity seems destined to be defined by management (and most co-workers) as superficial and hence inappropriate in the workplace.

As with the family we lack research specifically focused on the relationship of work and casual leisure as well as work and project-based leisure. It is hard to imagine employers being as generous as the ones McQuarrie studied, were their employees to ask for time off to, for instance, spend an afternoon at the beach, take in the local community fair, or even engage in some middle- or high-brow reading. But, from the point of view of the typical employee, casual leisure may well look better than the job this person must hold to maintain personal economic existence. Beauschesne (2005) reports data from a Workopolis poll indicating that nearly one in five Canadian employees dread going to work, while another three in five feel their employment is merely a job, a significantly disagreeable obligation. Belbin's (2003) set of interviews with working-age women who had left the workforce, considered with the Workopolis data, suggest that leisure, when juxtaposed with most work, seems for many people to be the more appealing of the two. For the majority of these people, this leisure is of the casual variety, since serious leisure is estimated not to be widespread (Stebbins, 1992, pp. 125–26).[6] Project-based leisure is possibly more sympathetically viewed, providing however, that it is one-shot volunteering (e.g., at a used book sale, a literary festival) or other activity having obvious benefit for the local community.

Gender

Generalizing from previous studies conducted in Canada and the United States, Ross says that "heavy readers are more likely to be female than male; to be younger rather than older; and to have achieved a higher educational level than the population at large" (Ross, 1999, p. 786). Of the 194 people she interviewed for her study, 65 percent were female and 35 percent were male. These are presumably people who read for pleasure or self-fulfillment, since she failed to examine the utilitarian motive for reading. Furthermore, utilitarian reading may not have an unequal gender distribution directly related to preference for it. If such a pattern exists (here research is scattered), it would be related to more distal factors such as which sex is most likely to read textbooks in which courses, the research literature in which fields, the complicated instructions for which projects (e.g., the IKEA sofa-bed, making a dress).

The proposition has just been advanced that adult women are considerably more likely to read than adult men, an assertion that receives some further, albeit, indirect support with the founding of the Women's National Book Association (WNBA). Established in 1917, even before women in America had the right to vote, the WNBA is today a vibrant organization operating from its base in New York City. In 2007 it launched the National Reading Group Month whose mission is to

- Increase public awareness of the joy and value of shared reading.
- Provide a time for reading groups to celebrate their accomplishments and plan for the future.
- Provide opportunities for individuals to join an existing reading group or start a new one.
- Encourage libraries, bookstores, and organizations to host special reading group events.[7]

The WNBA came into existence to communicate with women about matters relevant to themselves and the world of books, fueled by the hope that these women would inform and help each another. These goals are still a priority, although the organization now serves both men and women who participate in this world.

Some serious leisure is gendered, of which committed reading stands as a leading example. Research on leisure activities pursued predominantly by one sex or the other is reasonably prevalent. For instance, King (2001) studied quilters, an essentially female hobby the products of which express the "women's voice" (see also Stalp, 2007).The same may be said for the hobby of knitting (Prigoda and McKenzie, 2007), the pursuit of belly dancing (Kraus, 2010), and the diverse leisure activities enjoyed through active membership in the all-female Red Hat Society (Yarnal et al., 2008). On the male side, skydiving and gun collecting attract mostly men as do the leisure manifestations of do-it-yourself (Gelber, 1997) and juvenile auto theft (Drozda, 2006). Nevertheless, most serious leisure today is the province of both sexes, even while some of it is pursued in same-sex groups as rugby, basketball, and barbershop singing are.

The Wider Community

Serious leisure participants sometimes make culturally enriching contributions to their local community (see Stebbins, 2007a, chap. 4). Thus, the local civic orchestra provides it with classical music and the local astronomy club may offer an annual "star night" for public exploration of the heavens observed through the telescopes of members. And the town's model railroaders sometimes mount for popular viewing exhibitions of the fruits of their hobby. Local book fairs (or festivals), author readings, and book launchings perform a similar communal function made possible by committed readers, although invariably with some sponsorial help from nearby book sellers and the publishing industry.[8]

A still broader contribution to the community (and sometimes even the larger society) can come from pursuing serious leisure activities as well as some project-based leisure. This contribution is known as "community involvement" or "civil labor." Community involvement is local voluntary action, where members of a local community participate together in nonprofit groups or other communal activities. Often the goal here is to improve community life (Smith et al., 2006). Civil labor, which is synonymous with community involvement, differs only in its emphasis on human activity that is devoted to unpaid renewal and expansion of social capital (Rojek, 2002, p. 21). Beck (2000, p. 125) says that civil labor comprises housework, family work, club work, and volunteer work. This is an extremely broad conception, however, which encompasses the wide field of unpaid work, or unpaid obligation.

Rojek (2002, pp. 26–27) argues that, for the most part, civil labor is the communal contribution that amateurs, hobbyists, and career volunteers make when they pursue their serious leisure. Civil labor, however conceived of, generates social capital, defined here as the connections among individuals manifested in social networks, trustworthiness, acts motivated by the norm of reciprocity, and the like that develop in a community or larger society (Putnam, 2000, p. 19). The concept is analogous to those of human capital and physical capital (e.g., natural resources, financial resources); it refers to the arrangement whereby human groups of all kinds benefit from and advance their interests according to the salutary interconnections of their members.

With one exception casual leisure appears not to make this kind of contribution to community. True, people are sometimes joined in such leisure with strangers, especially these days over the Internet. This also happens with *tribes* (Maffesoli, 1996), a concept introduced in the preceding chapter. Of note in the present chapter is the fact that tribes are special leisure organizations, special ways of organizing the pursuit of particular kinds of casual leisure. Tribes are also found in serious leisure,

Taste-based tribes (e.g., music, clothing)	Activity-based tribes: consumers (e.g., popular novel)	Activity-based tribes: buffs (e.g., StarTrek, soap opera)	Social Worlds of (e.g., amateurs, career volunteers)
LEAST			MOST
COMPLEX			COMPLEX
Casual leisure	Casual leisure	Serious leisure	Serious leisure

Figure 7.1.   Structural complexity: From tribes to social worlds. Adapted from R. A. Stebbins, The organizational basis of leisure participation: A motivation exploration. State College, PA: Venture, p. 70.

but not, however, in project-based leisure (see Stebbins, 2002, pp. 69–71). Tribes, social worlds, casual leisure, and serious leisure are related in figure 7.1.[9]

But no contribution is made to the community in the casual leisure just mentioned, tribal involvements included. Hence it may not be qualified as civil labor. The glaring exception here is, of course, casual volunteering; it is done expressly for this reason. And, in the course of doing it, volunteers may well meet and serve with people never before encountered, say, in routine helping out with author readings or launchings at a local book shop. This, too, is civil labor. So we may conclude that such labor is not limited to serious leisure and volunteer project-based leisure, but also finds its place in one vitally important type of casual leisure.

As for project-based leisure it offers at minimum two routes to enriched communal life. One, it can bring into contact people who otherwise have no reason to meet, or at least to meet frequently. Two, by way of event volunteering and other collective altruistic activity, it can contribute to carrying off social events and projects. In other words some project-based leisure (mostly one-shot volunteer projects, it appears) can also be conceived of as civil labor as just defined, suggesting further that such activity is not strictly limited to serious leisure. Committed readers volunteering on a casual basis at a local second-hand book sale or a book festival exemplify this kind of civil labor.

CONCLUSION

For some people committed reading has its warts, principal among them, sedentariness, eccentric image, and ordinariness (lack of glamour). Moreover, some people—censors and would-be censors—see certain readings and classes of readings as dangerous to self and society. Yet on the whole, reading's complexion is reasonably flawless, for it also shows a comely set of benefits and rewards.

In this respect committed reading, on its broadest plane, is positive activity, experienced in a serious pursuit (motivated by utilitarian or fulfilling ends) or in a casual interest (motivated by pleasure). Such reading can be part of what people do to create for themselves and (sometimes) for society a worthwhile existence that is, in combination, substantially rewarding, satisfying, and fulfilling. Additionally, several benefits of pleasurable reading were considered in chapter 4: serendipitous discoveries about oneself and the larger community; edutainment, or acquisition of knowledge while being entertained (e.g., through a historical novel); regeneration after a day's work or other demanding activity; development and maintenance of interpersonal relationships; and the generation of well-being and contribution to an optimal leisure lifestyle.

The positive returns from committed reading as a serious pursuit have been framed in this book using the language of rewards, a list of which was set out in chapter 2. Thus reading sought for utilitarian and self-fulfilling reasons can produce some deeply enriching experiences. This is not usually possible with manuals and pamphlets, but the content of some reports and that of all scientific articles and books provides a fine vehicle for intellectual enrichment. And enrichment is the obvious reward to be gained from reading belletristic works. Self-actualization comes with improvement in reading skills and with a sense of mastering a body of literature (i.e., understanding it in utilitarian reading, gaining familiarity with it in utilitarian and fulfilling reading). The reward of self-expression is felt when readers put their considerable skills into action reading a book or an article and when they have the opportunity to speak, write, or otherwise act authoritatively with reference to the corpus they know so well.

These three constitute the main rewards of most serious pursuits (Stebbins, 2007a), often summarized as having achieved self-fulfillment. The other rewards listed in chapter 2 are less consequential and, in the case of some of them, not even felt. Thus self-image as a committed reader carries rather little weight in today's world compared with that generated by some other serious pursuits in, for example, sports, art, entertainment, and in certain hobbies. Self-gratification often translates as the fun experienced while enacting a serious pursuit, a feeling that seems alien to committed reading. Still, fulfilling reading can refresh the reader much as pleasurable reading does.

Lastly, the possibility of financial return is irrelevant to all committed reading except some of that done in devotee work. Even here this reward is for the most part only indirectly experienced, as in conducting a thorough literature review whose excellence figures in the editorial decision to accept the article for publication. Later, this happy outcome may lead to a modest raise in salary. This raise will be more substantial should the fine "lit review" be part of a research monograph. Additionally, a much smaller number of readers are remunerated directly for evaluating book manuscripts and proposals, although the amount is token, grandly qualified as an "honorarium."

There are also three possible social rewards that may be experienced some of the time by some committed readers. Face-to-face discussion groups are socially attractive for those who like gatherings of this sort. The same can be said for readers who enjoy rubbing elbows with other enthusiasts at book fairs, launchings, and readings. Group accomplishment is rewarding for the (probably) small proportion of all committed readers who serve as volunteers at these events. Contributing to the maintenance and development of a collectivity would be a social reward for readers who, acting as volunteers, establish a discussion group or program of readings. In sum, committed reading delivers a powerful set of personal rewards to its participants, with some of them also realizing the occasional social reward. This latter category of reward, however, is of secondary importance for the vast majority.

The foregoing has painted committed readers in some rather special colors. Sure, there are many other leisure activities that can be primarily personally rewarding (e.g., playing the piano or guitar, working cross-word puzzles, painting or sketching, and collecting certain kinds of collectibles). But none has the configuration of rewards, benefits, and life-style (convenience, ease, affordability, threat, and environment, and social world) that characterizes committed reading. Furthermore, that such reading could be a catalyst for profound personal change is not to be taken lightly. Daniel Pennac, a French writer and recipient of the Prix Renaudot in 2007 for his essay "Chagrin d'école," must have had at least some of this picture in mind when he proposed the "Reader's Bill of Rights":

1. The right to not read
2. The right to skip pages
3. The right to not finish
4. The right to reread
5. The right to read anything
6. The right to escapism
7. The right to read anywhere
8. The right to browse
9. The right to read out loud
10. The right to not defend your tastes

We have not covered all these rights in this book. But the ones we have addressed ourselves to, however briefly, give substance to the argument made here that committed readers occupy a unique and important place in modern society. Hence, a bill of rights protecting their interests is quite in order.

NOTES

1. http://www.quoteland.com/topic/Reading-Quotes/122/?pg=6.

2. Some teachers who adopt textbooks for their courses also aspire to write one, based in part on their sense of a need for another approach to the subject at hand. They constitute a very special class of reader of this genre, however, with its main audience being the students whose assignment is to read these books.

3. Robert Byrne once remarked that "nobody ever committed suicide while reading a good book, but many have while trying to write one."

4. Source: http://www.guardian.co.uk/books/2009/may/26/hay-festival-book-changed-life.

5. Source: http://www.wholesomewords.org/biography/bbunyan.html. As for his change in habits, one that Bunyan abandoned was swearing. He was reputed to have in this colorful arena the richest of vocabularies, outdoing in unrestrained vulgarity even the most proficient of his mates.

6. Polson (2006) estimates that 15 to 25 percent of leisure participants engage in what we call "serious leisure."

7. http://www.wnba-books.org.

8. Local book fairs seem to revolve substantially around the sale of used books, and therefore differ both from the consumer-driven book festivals like the annual National Book Festival in Washington, DC, as well as from the big international, commercially driven book fairs held in such places as New York, Frankfurt, Delhi, Abu Dhabi, and London geared toward publishers, distributors, and booksellers.

9. Buffs and consumers are defined in chapter 2.

References

Ablow, R. (2007). *The marriage of minds: Reading sympathy in the Victorian marriage plot.* Palo Alto, CA: Stanford University Press.

Alini, E. (2009). No more perks: Coffee shops pull the plug on laptop users. *The Wall Street Journal,* 6 August, http://online.wsj.com/article/SB124950421033208823.html.

Alta Language Services (2009). The most beautiful words in English. http://www.altalang.com/beyond-words/2009/01/08/the-most-beautiful-words-in-english.

Alta Language Services (2010). The ugliest words in English. http://www.altalang.com/beyond-words/2010/04/15/the-ugliest-words-in-english.

Altheide, D. L., and Snow, R. P. (1991). *Media worlds in the postjournalism era.* Hawthorne, NY: Aldine de Gruyter.

Anderson, J., and Raine, L. (2010). Future of the Internet IV. *Pew Internet and American Life Project,* February 19, www.pewinternet.org/Reports/2010/Future-of-the-Internet-IV/Part-3Gadgets.aspx.

Anderson, R., Hiebert, E., Scott, J., and Wilkinson, I. (1985). *Becoming a nation of readers: Report of the Commission on Reading in the United States.* Washington, DC: National Academy of Education, National Institute of Education, and Center for the Study of Reading.

Arai, S. M., and Pedlar, A. M. (1997). Building communities through leisure: Citizen participation in a healthy communities initiative. *Journal of Leisure Research,* 29, 167–02.

Applebaum, H. (1992). *The concept of work: Ancient, medieval, and modern.* Albany, NY: State University of New York Press.

Bates, M. J. (1999). The invisible substrate of information science. *Journal of the American Society for Information Science,* 50(12), 1043–50.

Beauchesne, E. (2005). Hate your job? You're not alone. *Calgary Herald,* 2 September, p. E6.

Beck, U. (2000). *The brave new world of work,* trans. by P. Camiller. New York: Polity Press.

Belbin, L. (2003). The opt-out revolution. *New York Times Magazine,* 26 October, pp. 1–13.

Bosman, J. (2012a). The bookstore's last stand. *New York Times,* 28 January (online edition).

Bosman, J. (2012b). Discreetly digital, erotic novel sets American woman abuzz. *New York Times,* 9 March (online edition).

Bosman, J., and Richtel, M. (2012). Finding your book interrupted . . . by the tablet you read it on. *New York Times,* 4 March (online edition).

Boswell, R. (2011). Canadian trust museums over Internet facts. *Calgary Herald,* 26 December, p. A11 (Postmedia News release).

Bowen, C. D. (1935). *Friends and fiddlers.* Boston, MA: Little, Brown.

Brissett, D., and Snow, R. P. (1993). Boredom: Where the future isn't. *Symbolic Interaction,* 16, 237–56.

Brooks, D. (2007). The odyssey years. *New York Times,* 9 October (online edition).

Browning, D. (2012). Learning to love airport lit. *New York Times,* 17 February (online edition).

Bush, D. M., and Simmons, R. G. (1981). Socialization processes over the life course. In M. Rosenberg and R. H. Turner (Eds.), *Social psychology* (pp. 133–64). Brunswick, NJ: Transaction.

Butler, R. N. (1963). The life review: An interpretation of reminiscence in the aged. *Psychiatry*, 26, 65–76.

Carr, N. (2008). Is Google making us stupid? What the internet is doing to our brains. *Atlantic Monthly*, July/August, 302, 56–63.

Case, D. O. (2002). *Looking for information: A survey of research on information seeking, needs and behavior*. Amsterdam: Academic Press.

Case, D. O. (2009). Serial collecting as leisure, and coin collecting in particular. *Library Trends*, 57, 729–52.

Chang, S-J. L. (2009). Information research in leisure: Implications from an empirical study of backpackers. *Library Trends*, 57, 711–28.

Clark, C., and Rumbold, K. (2006). *Reading for pleasure: A research review*. London: National Literacy Trust.

ComScore Data Mine (2011). Average time spent online per U.S. visitor for 2010, 13 January, http://www.comscoredatamine.com/2011/01/average-time-spent-online-per-u-s-visitor-in-2010.

Cook, D. T. (2006). Leisure and consumption. In C. Rojek, S. M. Shaw, and A. J. Veal (Eds.), *A handbook of leisure studies* (pp. 304–16). New York: Palgrave Macmillan.

Csikszentmihalyi, M. (1990). *Flow: The psychology of optimal experience*. New York: Harper and Row.

Cullinan, B. E. (2000). Independent reading and school achievement. *School Library Media Research*, 3, http://www.ala.org/aasl/aaslpubsandjournals/slmrb/slmrcontents/volume32000/independent.

Dannefer, D. (1980). Rationality and passion in private experience: Modern consciousness and the social world of old-car collectors. *Social Problems*, 27, 392–412.

Davidson, L., and Stebbins, R. A. (2011). *Serious leisure and nature: Sustainable consumption in the outdoors*. Houndmills, Basingstoke, UK: Palgrave Macmillan.

de Bury, R. (1909). *The love of books: The philobiblon of Richard de Bury*, trans. by E. C. Thomas. London: Chatto and Windus.

Delamere, F. M., and Shaw, S. M. (2006). Playing with violence: Gamers' social construction of violent video game play as tolerable deviance. *Leisure/Loisir*, 30, 7–26.

Department of Culture, Media and Sport (2010). *Taking part: The national survey of culture, leisure and sport, adult and child report 2009/10*. London: Government of the United Kingdom, http://www.culture.gov.uk/images/research/TakingPart_AdultChild2009–10_StatisticalRelease.pdf.

Drozda, C. (2006). Juveniles performing auto theft: An exploratory study into a deviant leisure lifestyle. *Leisure/Loisir*, 30, 111–32.

Dubin, R. (1992). *Central life interests: Creative individualism in a complex world*. New Brunswick, NJ: Transaction.

The Economist (2005). Up off the couch. 22 October, p. 35.

The Economist (2006). The land of pleasure. 4 February, www.economist.com.

The Economist (2012a). The east is read. 10 March, p. 56.

The Economist (2012b). Of brooms and bondage. 5 May, p. 66.

Elgin, D. (1981). *Voluntary simplicity: Toward a way of life that is outwardly simple, inwardly rich*. New York: William Morrow.

Ewoudou, J. (2005). *Understanding culture consumption in Canada* (Catalogue no. 81–595–M No. 066). Ottawa, ON: Statistics Canada, Government of Canada.

Fischer, G., and Scharff, E. (1998). Learning technologies in support of self-directed learning. *Journal of Interactive Media in Education*, North America, Oct. 1998. Available at http://www-jime.open.ac.uk/article/1998–4/26.

Fisher, B., Day, M., and Collier, C. (1998). Successful aging: Volunteerism and generativity in later life. In D. Redburn and R. McNamara (Eds.), *Social gerontology* (pp. 43–54). Westport, CT: Auburn.

Fullagar, S., and Owler, K. (1998). Narratives of leisure: Recreating the self. *Disability and Society*, 13, 441–450.

Gallagher, K. (2009). *Readicide: How schools are killing reading and what you can do about*. Portland, ME: Stenhouse.

Garner, D. (2012). Miniature e-books let journalists stretch legs. *New York Times*, 6 March (online edition)

Gelber, S. M. (1997). Do-it-yourself: Constructing, repairing and maintaining domestic masculinity. *American Quarterly*, 49(1), 66–112.

Gerson, J. (2010). Video games keep kids fit. *Calgary Herald*, 8 December, B1.

Gioia, D. (2007). Preface. *To read or not to read: A question of national consequence* (executive summary). Washington, DC: National Endowment for the Arts.

Goffman, E. (1963). *Stigma: Notes on the management of spoiled identity*. Englewood Cliffs, NJ: Prentice-Hall.

Greaney, V. (1980). Factors related to amount and type of leisure reading. *Reading Research Quarterly*, 15, 337–57.

Gunn, L., and Cassie, L. T. (2006). Serial murder as an act of deviant leisure. *Leisure/ Loisir*, 30, 27–53.

Hamilton-Smith, E. (1971). The preparation of volunteer workers with adolescent groups. *Australian Social Work*, 24 (3 and 4), 26–33.

Harrison, N., and Gravelle, F. (2008).The importance of leisure when living with a life threatening disease: From a serious leisure perspective. *International Journal of Sport Management, Recreation, and Tourism*, 2, 38–46.

Hartel, J. (2003). The serious leisure frontier in library and information science: Hobby domains. *Knowledge Organization*, 30(3/4), 228–38.

Hartel, J. (2006). Information activities and resources in an episode of gourmet cooking. *Information Research*, 12(1), http://InformationR.net/ir/12–1/paper282.html.

Hartel, J. (2010). Managing documents at home for serious leisure: A case study of the hobby of gourmet cooking. *Journal of Documentation*, 66(6), 847–74.

Hassan, R. (2012). *The age of distraction: Reading, writing, and the politics in a high-speed networked economy*. New Brunswick, NJ: Transaction.

Heuser, L. (2005). We're not too old to play sports: The career of women lawn bowlers. *Leisure Studies*, 24, 45–60.

Houle, C. O. (1961). *The inquiring mind* Madison: University of Wisconsin Press.

Hutchinson, S. L., and Kleiber, D. A. (2005). Gifts of the ordinary: Casual leisure's contributions to health and well-being. *World Leisure Journal*, 47(3), 2–16.

Institute of Museum and Library Services (2011). *Public libraries survey fiscal year 2009*. Washington, DC.

Jackson, E. L. (Ed.) (2005). *Constraints to Leisure*. State College, PA: Venture Publishing.

Jacobs, A. (2011). *The pleasures of reading in an age of distraction*. New York: Oxford University Press.

Jarvis, P. (1995). *Adult and continuing education* (2nd ed.). London: Routledge.

Jeffries, V., Johnston, B. V., Nichols, L. T., Oliner, S. P., Tiryakian, E., and Weinstein, J. (2006). Altruism and social solidarity: Envisioning a field of specialization. *American Sociologist*, 37(3), 67–83.

Jones, I., and Symon, G. (2001). Lifelong learning as serious leisure: Policy, practice, and potential. *Leisure Studies*, 20, 269–84.

Jong, E. (2003). Close encounters of the reading kind. *Oprah Magazine*, August, 124.

Judson, O. (2010). Stand up while you read this. *New York Times*, 23 February (online edition).

Kaplan, M. (1960). *Leisure in America: A social inquiry*. New York: John Wiley.

Keen, Andrew (2007). *The cult of the amateur: How blogs, MySpace, YouTube, and the rest of today's user-generated media are destroying our economy, our culture, and our values*. London: Nicholas Brealey.

Kellogg, C. (2012). Social network e-reading coming to app near you. *The Calgary Herald*, 8 January, C2 (reprinted from the *Los Angeles Times*).

Kelly, M. (2012). Strategies for educators: Censorship and book banning, http://712educators.about.com/cs/bannedbooks/a/bookbanning_2.htm.

Kernan, A. (1992). *The death of literature*. New Haven, CT: Yale University Press.

King, F. L. (2001). Social dynamics of quilting, *World Leisure Journal*, 43(2), 26–29.

Krashen, S. (2004). *The power of reading*. Portsmouth: Heinemann and Westport, CT: Libraries Unlimited.

Kulish, N., and Bronner, E. (2012). Storm continues after German writer's poem against Israel. *New York Times*, 6 April (online edition).

Lambdin, L. (1997). *Elderlearning*. Phoenix, AZ: Oryx Press.

Laslett, P. (1994). The third age, the fourth age and the future. *Aging and Society*, 14, 436–47.

Lewis G. H. (1978). The sociology of popular culture. *Current Sociology*, 26 (Winter), 1–160.

Lewis, L. S., and Brissett, D. (1981). Paradise on demand. *Society*, 18 (July/August), 85–90.

Lumos Research, Inc. (2011). *An analysis of public library trends* (prepared for the Canadian Urban Libraries Council). Oakville, ON, http://www.culc.ca/cms_lib/CULC%20Public%20Library%20Trends-es.pdf.

Luyt, B., and Ho, S. A. (2011). Reading, the library, and the elderly: A Singapore case study. *Journal of Librarianship and Information Science*, 43(4), 204–12.

Maffesoli, M. (1996). *The time of the tribes: The decline of individualism*, trans. by D. Smith. London: Sage Publications.

Mann, S. J. (2000). The student's experience of reading. *Higher Education*, 39, 297–317.

Manning, P. K. (1999). High-risk narratives: Textual adventures. *Qualitative Sociology*, 22, 285–99.

Manzo, A.V., and Manzo, U. C. (1995). *Teaching children to be literate: A reflective approach*. New York: Harcourt Brace.

McMillion, B., Cutchins, D., Geissinger, A., and Asner, E. (2012). *Volunteer vacations: Short-term adventures that will benefit you and others*, 11th ed. Chicago: Chicago Review Press.

McQuarrie, F. A. E. (1999). An investigation of the effects of workplace support for serious leisure. *Proceedings of the 9th Canadian Congress on Leisure Research*. Wolfville, NS: Acadia University.

McQuarrie, F. A. E. (2000). Work careers and serious leisure: The effects of nonwork commitment on career commitment. *Leisure/Loisir*, 24, 115–38.

Muñoz, S. S. (2006). In clubs and online, hobbyists embrace the joys of picking. *Wall Street Journal*, 28 October, A1.

Munro, T. (1957). Four hundred arts and types of art. *Journal of Aesthetics and Art Criticism*, 16, 44–65.

National Endowment for the Arts (2007). *To read or not to read: A question of national consequence* (executive summary). Washington, DC: National Endowment for the Arts.

Nell, V. (1988). The psychology of reading for pleasure: Needs and gratifications. *Reading Research Quarterly*, 23, 6–50.

New World Encyclopedia (2008). Edutainment. http://www.newworldencyclopedia.org/entry/Edutainment.

Ogas, O. (2011). The online world of female desire. *Wall Street Journal*, 30 April (online edition).

Ogrodnik, L. (2000). *Patterns in culture consumption and participation*. Ottawa, ON: Statistics Canada, Government of Canada.

Olmsted, A. D. (1993). Hobbies and serious leisure. *World Leisure and Recreation*, 35 (Spring), 27–32.

Pettigrew, K. E., Fidel, R., and Bruce, H. (2001). Conceptual frameworks in information behavior. *Annual Review of Information Science and Technology (ARIST)*, 34, 43–78.

Pieper, J. (1963). *Leisure: The basis of culture*, trans. by A. Dru. New York: New American Library.

Polson, G. (2006). Leisure alternatives funnel chart. http://www.strengthtech.com/misc/funnel/funnel.htm.

Poortinga, W., Gebel, K., Bauman, A., and Moudon, A. V. (2011). Neighborhood environment, physical activity and obesity. In J. O. *Nriagu* (Ed.), *Encyclopedia of Environmental Health* (pp. 44–53). Amsterdam: Elsevier.

Prigoda, E., and McKenzie, P. J. (2007). Purls of wisdom: A collectivist study of human information behaviour in a public library knitting group. *Human Information Behavior*, 63, 90–114.

Principal Financial Services (2004). The principal global financial well-being survey: 2004 executive summary. Des Moines, IA: Principal Life Insurance Co.

Prose, F. (2009). *Reading like a writer: A guide for people who love books and for those who want to write them*. New York: HarperCollins.

Putnam, R. D. (2000). *Bowling alone: The collapse and revival of American community*. New York: Simon and Schuster.

Radway, J. A. (1999). *A feeling for books: The Book-of-the-Month Club, literary taste, and middle-class desire*. Chapel Hill: University of North Carolina Press.

Rane-Szostak, D., and Herth, K. A. (1995). Pleasure reading and other activities and loneliness in later life. *Journal of Adolescent and Adult Literacy*, 39, 100–06.

Rapoport, R. N., and Rapoport, R. (1975). *Leisure and the family life cycle*. London: Routledge and Kegan Paul.

Rawsthorn, A. (2012). The beauty of the printed book. *New York Times*, 12 February (online edition).

Roberson, D. N., Jr. (2005). Leisure and learning: An investigation of older adults and self-directed learning. *Leisure/Loisir*, 29, 203–38.

Rojek, C. (2002). Civil labour, leisure and post work society. *Société et Loisir/Society and Leisure*, 25, 21–36.

Ross, C. S. (1999). Finding without seeking: The information encounter in the context of reading for pleasure. *Information Processing and Management*, 35, 783–99.

Sabelis, I. (2004). Global Speed: A time view on transnationality. *Cultural and Organization*, 10(4), 291–301.

Sanders, B. (1994). *A Is for Ox: Violence, electronic media, and the silencing of the written word*. New York: Pantheon.

Selman, G., Selman, M., Cooke, M., and Dampier, P. (1998). *The foundations of adult education in Canada*, 2nd ed. Toronto: Thompson.

Shannon, V. (2007). 15 years of text messages, a "cultural phenomenon." *New York Times*, 5 December (online edition).

Siegenthaler, K. L., and O'Dell, I. (2003). Older golfers: Serious leisure and successful aging. *World Leisure Journal*, 45(1), 45–52.

Silverman, M. A. (2006). Beyond fun in games: The serious leisure of the power gamer. Master's Dissertation, Department of Sociology, Concordia University.

Simmel, G. (1949). The sociology of sociability. *American Journal of Sociology*, 55, 254–61.

Smith, D. H., Stebbins, R. A., and Dover, M. (2006). *A dictionary of nonprofit terms and concepts*. Bloomington: Indiana University Press.

Snyder, C. R., and Lopez, J. (2007). *Positive psychology: The scientific and practical explorations of human strengths*. Thousand Oaks, CA: Sage.

Stalp, M. B. (2007). *Quilting: The fabric of everyday life*. New York: Berg.

Statistics Canada (2011). *The Canada yearbook 2011* (catalogue no. 11–402–X). Ottawa, ON: Government of Canada.

Stebbins, R. A. (1970). Career: The subjective approach. *The Sociological Quarterly*, 11, 32–49.

Stebbins, R. A. (1980). Avocational science: The amateur routine in archaeology and astronomy, *International Journal of Comparative Sociology*, 21, 34–48.

Stebbins, R. A. (1982). Serious leisure: A conceptual statement. *Pacific Sociological Review*, 25, 251–72.

Stebbins, R. A. (1990). *The laugh-makers: Stand-up comedy as art, business, and life-style*. Montréal: McGill-Queen's University Press.

Stebbins, R. A. (1992). *Amateurs, professionals, and serious leisure*. Montreal: McGill-Queen's University Press.

Stebbins, R. A. (1993a). *Canadian football. A view from the helmet.* (reprinted ed.). Toronto: Canadian Scholars Press.

Stebbins, R. A. (1993b). *Career, culture and social psychology in a variety art: The magician* (reprinted ed.). Malabar, FL: Krieger.

Stebbins, R. A. (1994). The liberal arts hobbies: A neglected subtype of serious leisure. *Loisir et Société/Society and Leisure,* 16, 173–86.

Stebbins, R. A. (1996a). *The barbershop singer: Inside the social world of a musical hobby.* Toronto: University of Toronto Press.

Stebbins, R. A. (1996b). Volunteering: A serious leisure perspective. *Nonprofit and Voluntary Action Quarterly,* 25, 211–24.

Stebbins, R. A. (1998). *After work: The search for an optimal leisure lifestyle.* Calgary, AB: Detselig. (Also available at www.seriousleisure.net, Digital Library, Books.)

Stebbins, R. A. (2000). Optimal leisure lifestyle: Combining serious and casual leisure for personal well-being. In M. C. Cabeza (Ed.), *Leisure and human development: Proposals for the 6th World Leisure Congress* (pp. 101–07). Bilbao, Spain: University of Deusto.

Stebbins, R. A. (2001a). *New directions in the theory and research of serious leisure,* Mellen Studies in Sociology, vol. 28. Lewiston, NY: Edwin Mellen.

Stebbins, R. A. (2001b). Volunteering—mainstream and marginal: Preserving the leisure experience. In M. Graham and M. Foley (Eds.), *Volunteering in leisure: Marginal or inclusive?* (Vol. 75, pp. 1–10). Eastbourne, UK: Leisure Studies Association.

Stebbins, R. A. (2001c). *Exploratory research in the social sciences.* Thousand Oaks, CA: Sage.

Stebbins, R. A. (2002). *The organizational basis of leisure participation: A motivational exploration.* State College, PA: Venture Publishing.

Stebbins, R. A. (2004a). *Between work and leisure: The common ground of two separate worlds.* New Brunswick, NJ: Transaction.

Stebbins, R. A. (2004b). Pleasurable aerobic activity: A type of casual leisure with salubrious implications. *World Leisure Journal,* 46(4), 55–58. (Also available at www.seriousleisure.net, Digital Library, Other Works.)

Stebbins, R. A. (2005a). Project-based leisure: Theoretical neglect of a common use of free time. *Leisure Studies,* 24, 1–11.

Stebbins, R. A. (2005b). *Challenging mountain nature: Risk, motive, and lifestyle in three hobbyist sports.* Calgary, AB: Detselig. (Also available at www.seriousleisure.net, Digital Library/Books.)

Stebbins, R. A. (2006). Discretionary time commitment: Effects on leisure choice and lifestyle. *Leisure Studies Association Newsletter,* 74 (July), 18–20. (Also available at www.seriousleisure.net, Digital Library, "Leisure Reflections No. 12.")

Stebbins, R. A. (2007a). *Serious leisure: A perspective for our time.* New Brunswick, NJ: Transaction.

Stebbins, R. A. (2007b). A leisure-based, theoretic typology of volunteers and volunteering. *Leisure Studies Association Newsletter,* 78 (November), 9–12. (Also available at www.seriousleisure.net, Digital Library, "Leisure Reflections No. 16.")

Stebbins, R. A. (2009a). *Personal decisions in the public square: Beyond problem solving into a positive sociology.* New Brunswick, NJ: Transaction.

Stebbins, R. A. (2009b). *Leisure and consumption: Common ground, separate worlds.* New York: Palgrave Macmillan.

Stebbins, R. A. (2010). Flow in serious leisure: Nature and prevalence."*Leisure Studies Association Newsletter,* 87 (November), 21–23. (Also available at www.seriousleisure. net, Digital Library, "Leisure Reflections No. 25.")

Stebbins, R. A. (2011a). Personal memoirs, project-based leisure and therapeutic recreation for seniors. *Leisure Studies Association Newsletter,* 88 (March), 29–31. (Also available at www.seriousleisure.net, Digital Library, "Leisure Reflections No. 26.")

Stebbins, R. A. (2011b). Loisirs sérieux : Un exposé conceptuel. In A. Degenne, C, Marry, and S. Moulin (Eds.), *Les catégories sociales et leurs frontières* (pp. 121–46). Québec, QC : Les Presses de l'Université Laval.

Stebbins, R. A. (2012). *The idea of leisure: First principles*. New Brunswick, NJ: Transaction.

Stebbins, R. A. (2013). *Work and leisure in the Middle East: The common ground of two separate worlds*. New Brunswick, NJ: Transaction.

Streitfeld, D. (2011). Foreclosed homeowners go to court on their own. *New York Times*, 2 February (online edition).

Styles, C. (2007). Library-based adult reading for pleasure in the USA and the Netherlands: Transferable lessons for English public libraries, http://www.cloreleadership. org/~clorelea/cms/user_files/fellow_fellowship_research_projects_download_ report/33/Claire%20Styles%20Clore%20Research%202007.pdf.

Swartz, J. (2010). Time spent on Facebook, Twitter, YouTube grows. *USA Today*, 2 August (online edition).

UNESCO (1976). *Recommendation on the development of adult education*. Paris.

Unruh, D. R. (1979). Characteristics and types of participation in social worlds. *Symbolic Interaction*, 2, 115–30.

Unruh, D. R. (1980). The nature of social worlds. *Pacific Sociological Review*, 23, 271–96.

U.S. Census Bureau (2000). *Statistical Abstract of the United States* (119th ed.). Washington, DC.

U.S. Census Bureau (2010). *Statistical Abstract of the United States* (129th ed.). Washington, DC.

Veblen, T. (1953). *The theory of the leisure class*. New York: New American Library.

Wearing, B., and Fullager, S. (1996). The ambiguity in Australian women's family leisure: Some figures and refiguring. In N. Samuel (Ed.), *Women, leisure and the family in contemporary society: A multinational Perspective* (pp. 15–34). Wallingford, Oxon, UK: CABI Publishing.

Williams, R. M., Jr. (2000). American society. In E. F. Borgatta and R. J. V. Montgomery (Eds.), *Encyclopedia of sociology*, 2nd ed., Vol. 1 (pp. 140–48). New York: Macmillan.

Wilson, T. D. (1999). Models in information behaviour research. *Journal of Documentation*, 55 (3), 249–70.

Wuthnow, R. (2007). *After the baby boomers. How the twenty- and thirty-somethings are shaping the future of American religion*. Princeton, NJ: Princeton University Press.

Yarnal, C. M., Chick, G., and Kerstetter, D. L. (2008). I did not have time to play growing up . . . so this is my play time. It's the best thing I have ever done for myself: What is play to older women? *Leisure Sciences*, 30, 235–52.

Yiannakis, A., and Gibson, H. (1992). Roles tourists play. *Annals of Tourism Research*, 19, 287–303.

Yoder, D. G. (1997). A model for commodity intensive serious leisure. *Journal of Leisure Research*, 29, 407–29.

Index

About the Author

Robert A. Stebbins, FRSC, is faculty professor in the Department of Sociology at the University of Calgary. He received his Ph.D. in 1964 from the University of Minnesota. He has written over 225 articles and chapters and written or edited 41 books, including, recently, *Serious Leisure: A Perspective for Our Time* (2007) and *Personal Decisions in the Public Square: Beyond Problem Solving into a Positive Sociology* and *Leisure and Consumption: Common Ground/Separate Worlds*, both published in 2009. His *Social Entrepreneurship for Dummies* (with Mark Durieux) was published in 2010, and his monograph (with Lee Davidson) on nature-challenge activities, *Serious Leisure and Nature: Sustainable Consumption in the Outdoors*, was published in 2011. His volume *The Idea of Leisure: First Principles* was released in early 2012, and *Work and Leisure in the Middle East: The Common Ground of Two Separate Worlds* will be available in early 2013.

Stebbins's most recent research and writing interests center on volunteering among the elderly, leisure education, and leisure as the basis for personal distinctiveness. Stebbins was elected fellow of the Academy of Leisure Sciences in 1996, the Royal Society of Canada in 1999, and the World Leisure Academy in 2010. He is also an elected alumni member of the Phi Beta Kappa Society, Macalester College Chapter. His interests in leisure studies stretch back to late 1973 with research on amateurs in music, theater, archaeology, and baseball. He and Jenna Hartel maintain the serious leisure perspective website (www.seriousleisure.net), which they inaugurated in 2006.